The Commercial Club

INDIANAPOLIS FIRST

By George and Miriam Geib

FOUNDING MEMBERS

Eli Lilly and Company
INB National Bank
The Indianapolis News

Market Street, West from Monument

MARION COUNTY COURT HOUSE (TOMLINSON HALL & CITY MARKET AT LEFT), INDIANAPOLIS, IND.

Emrichsville Bridge, Ind.

7383

INDIANAPOLIS
The Speedway City
FOR HOOSIER HOSPITALITY

D edicated to the founders and members of the Commercial Club and its successor, the Indianapolis Chamber of Commerce, whose concern, forethought, vision, and energetic activity have allowed Indianapolis to experience the energy and accomplishment of urban excellence. We particularly pay tribute to three of our founders—Eli Lilly and Company, INB National Bank, and The Indianapolis News—which remain committed to the Chamber 100 years after its birth.

INDIANAPOLIS FIRST
A Commemorative History
of the
Indianapolis Chamber of Commerce
and the
Local Business Community

By
George and Miriam Geib

Published by the Indianapolis Chamber of Commerce
320 North Meridian Street, Indianapolis, IN 46204
© 1990 All Rights Reserved

ISBN 0-9627335-0-4
Library of Congress Catalogue Card Number: 90-83335

Sponsored by:
The Associated Group; Baker & Daniels; BANK ONE, INDIANAPOLIS, NA; Barnes & Thornburg; Business Furniture Corporation; Citizens Gas & Coke Utility; Community Hospitals Indianapolis; Ice Miller Donadio and Ryan; INB National Bank; The Indianapolis News; Indianapolis Power and Light Company; Jenn-Air Company; Lacy Diversified Industries, Ltd.; Eli Lilly and Company; Marsh Supermarkets; Merchants National Bank and Trust Company; Park Fletcher, Inc.; Railroadmen's Federal Savings and Loan Association; Ransburg Corporation; St. Francis Hospital Center; St. Vincent Hospital and Health Care Center; Union Federal Savings Bank and Walker Research, Inc.

Publisher
Thomas A. King

Project Director
Daniel Fenton

Designer
Richard Listenberger
Listenberger Design Associates

Photo Editor
Melba Hopper

Project Manager
Lauri Hogan

Editorial Advisory Board
Carl Dortch (Chair)
James Farmer
Carl Henn
Anita Martin
Frank Hoke

Editorial Assistant
Kelli Riley

Photo Research Assistant
Jennifer Kain

Jacket and Primary
Color Photography
McGuire Studios, Inc.

Contents

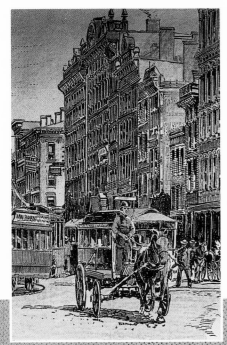

Introduction

For one hundred years, the Indianapolis Chamber of Commerce has been the voice of the business community in the Circle City. The organization was founded as the Indianapolis Commercial Club in 1890. It assumed its new title in 1912 when it merged with the other principal organizations that spoke for wholesale and retail trade, manufacturing, and shipping in Marion County.

The Chamber has sought from its founding to create a community that would be attractive to current and future business ventures. The group was early recognized as a national leader in promoting the *scientific* search for growth and expansion, carefully seeking businesses that would be able to succeed and prosper in the Indianapolis environment and vigorously searching for customers and contractors for local products and services. Much of the activity has been the quiet work of gathering statistics, distributing information, and developing personal networks among business leaders.

The Chamber has also been a leader in promoting civic activities that would make Indianapolis an attractive community in which to live. Projects ranging from public health to education renewal have absorbed members'

interests and commitment and have left a wide variety of visible and organizational legacies. Humanitarian activities have often occurred well in advance of national trends. Governmental activities have frequently called public and private interests into partnership. The Chamber has thus been a vigorous advocate of the American enterprise system. Modern Indianapolis stands as a measure of its success.

This centennial history of the Chamber is a record of its activities, ideals, and accomplishments. The story begins with Col. Eli Lilly and twenty-six other business leaders who met at the Bates House in 1890 to form a group that could help to give direction to the commercial needs of a rapidly expanding industrial city. Their early activities—striving to create efficient and responsive city government, improve local transportation, and articulate and implement a vision of a *city beautiful*—form the context of the opening chapter.

These activities were often tied to a humanitarian spirit that guided leadership in situations as varied as vocational education and the 1913 flood. The spirit that these activities exemplified reappears in the Chamber's commercial activities, ranging from the development of an industrial suburb to support for war industry in World War I.

With the 1920s, the Chamber's history becomes increasingly tied to the new manufacturing and retail enterprises of the city. Soaring membership, an expanded professional staff, and a desire to establish Indianapolis as a leader in light industry combined to make the decade a golden one of projects and initiatives.

The Chamber proved able to withstand the challenges of depression as well. Its relief efforts in the early 1930s, and its attempts to expand the transportation base of the city thereafter, showed a vigor that it carried into the industrial activities of World War II. Its firmly held commitments also made it a strong advocate of the enterprise system in the decades after the war.

These activities were regularly joined with a concern for the health of the community, a concern expressed in the Chamber's interests in public housing, education, employment opportunities, and initiatives to promote city-county cooperation. The group worked in active partnership with other civic organizations to realize the potential of unified metropolitan government, particularly in such joint public-private ventures as planning for amateur and professional athletics in the city. The story of the urban renaissance of the last twenty-five years cannot be told without reference to the Chamber.

The key measure of the Chamber's success is that it has been able to understand and serve the changing commercial needs of the city, attracting to its ranks and to its leadership positions business leaders whose energy and ideas have shaped its messages and programs. This centennial history is a record of those people and their visions, a record of informed public and private partnership.

Top: Washington Street looking east from Meridian Street, circa 1860. The need for concerted efforts to improve and pave city streets motivated twenty-seven business and civic leaders to organize the Commercial Club in 1890.

Bottom: A natural gas boom began in Indianapolis in 1887 when Omer Boardmen heated and cooked with gas drilled from a well across the street from his home near Broad Ripple. Gas main construction, shown here in a Blackford County scene, was one sign of urban growth problems in the late 1800s.

Chapter 1

The Founding Years

The beginnings were both proud and humble. The pride was for a new city of the American West that, in less than seventy years, had vaulted from an "overgrown country town" to one of America's twenty-five largest cities. The humility came from the recognition that growth had brought with it severe urban problems. Railroad development, industrial expansion, and housing construction all created challenges. But none were more obtrusive or annoying than the piles of dirt that Jacob Dunn, in his *History of Greater Indianapolis,* called "miniature mountain ranges" along most of the streets. They had been left by two competing natural gas companies as they raced to lay their mains through the settled areas of the city, heedless of the damages they inflicted on the public thoroughfares. So troubling was the problem that it provoked a call to public action, and a bold response that has shaped Indianapolis for a hundred years.

The response reflected a new vision of the possibilities of urban life, a vision widely articulated across America in the late nineteenth century. This vision, often called "progressive" by contemporary reformers and later historians, portrayed the city as a physical expression of community ideals and values, a setting that both reflected and contributed to the moral and intellectual growth of each citizen.

A "Boomer" Spirit

Many Indianapolis leaders were attracted to the vision, and were thus in need of an effective means of mobilizing civic and business support to achieve their goals and reforms. Urban experiences in other major cities, moreover, suggested that a chamber of commerce was a particularly good means to those ends. Such chambers, under various names, had appeared in many American cities during the nineteenth century, striving to unite the leadership of the business community behind the promotion of their city and region. Led by members called "boomers" (a label changed to "boosters" in the twentieth century), these early chambers had motives that varied from disinterested altruism to aggressive self-interest. Their methods invariably involved activities to attract new investors, new industries, and new citizens. As *The Indianapolis News* put it in January 1890,

> Boom it. Boom the factory . . . boom the town. Can not Indianapolis accomplish something? Let us borrow some Chicago snap if we have none of our own.

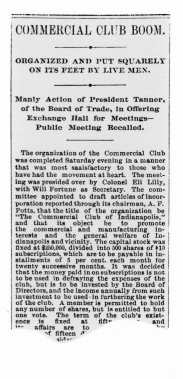

BOOM IT!

The Indianapolis News confirmed the formation of the Commercial Club in a front page story the Monday following the group's organization on February 8, 1890. Just one week earlier, the paper ran editorials calling for an organization that would lead Indianapolis on the road to prosperity.

COMMERCIAL CLUB BOOM.

ORGANIZED AND PUT SQUARELY ON ITS FEET BY LIVE MEN.

Manly Action of President Tanner, of the Board of Trade, in Offering Exchange Hall for Meetings— Public Meeting Recalled.

The organization of the Commercial Club was completed Saturday evening in a manner that was most saaisfactory to those who have had the movement at heart. The meeting was presided over by Colonel Eli Lilly, with Will Fortune as Secretary. The committee appointed to draft articles of incorporation reported through its chairman, A. F. Potts, that the title of the organization be "The Commercial Club of Indianapolis," and that its object be to promote the commercial and manufacturing interests and the general welfare of Indianapolis and vicinity. The capital stock was fixed at $250,000, divided into 500 shares of $19 subscriptions, which are to be payable in installments of 5 per cent. each month for twenty successive months. It was decided that the money paid in on subscriptions is not to be used in defraying the expenses of the club, but is to be invested by the Board of Directors, and the income annually from such investment to be used - in furthering the work of the club. A member is permitted to hold any number of shares, but is entitled to but one vote. The term of the club's existence is fixed at fift— and ... affairs are to ... of fifteen ...

11

The corner of Washington Street and Illinois Street, a historic hotel site, has been home to a rustic log inn, the Bates House, the Claypool Hotel, and the Embassy Suites Hotel. City leaders met at the Bates House in 1890 to organize the Commercial Club of Indianapolis.

Earlier Chambers and Boards

As *The News* implied, however, chambers of commerce had not enjoyed the same record in Indianapolis that was common in other cities. At least five attempts were made to organize or reorganize a group; all met with only limited success. In 1853, for example, the desire to promote railroad development led to the creation of a Board of Trade which folded after barely a year of meetings. Three years later a second Board reorganized to circulate information regarding the location of new businesses in the city and enjoyed some success during the boom times of the Civil War.

In 1864 the Board was joined by the first city Chamber of Commerce, under the leadership of T. B. Elliott, president, and Jehial Barnard, secretary, which engaged in business "agitation," or promotion, in the next few years. In 1868 they stimulated the organization of a Merchants and Manufacturing Association designed to promote cooperation between retailers and manufacturers. Two years later the Board of Trade reorganized again to absorb the activities of the Chamber and the Association, and in 1873 it took the major step of erecting its own building at the southeast corner of Maryland and Capitol.

In addition to its avowed purpose of promoting trade, the building was designed to provide rental space that could give the Board a reliable income. It was built by a subsidiary company called the Indianapolis Chamber of Commerce and was called, confusingly, both the Board of Trade Building and the Chamber Building for many years.

Beyond erecting its building, however, the Board was not terribly active in the two decades after its 1870 reorganization. Local commentators invariably attributed this inactivity to the lingering effects of the great business depression called the Panic of 1873. This depression struck Indianapolis with savage intensity, reaching its greatest depths in the winter of 1878-79. In the process it halted a major period of real estate investment and speculation. Many local leaders had followed a path common to expanding cities by taking out mortgages to purchase, subdivide, and re-sell extensive suburban tracts.

Banks and savings and loan associations in Indianapolis had fueled this activity by readily granting loans, only to discover that the depression put an effective halt to land purchases. Personal fortunes soon disappeared as mortgages became due. Several bank failures followed by 1882. As Jacob Dunn's *History of Greater Indianapolis* summarized the problem, "All business activity was dull and demand for money for anything but paying debts was light."

Even more serious was the effect upon leadership attitudes in the city. With many personal fortunes lost or sadly eroded, it was difficult to find the families of ostentatious wealth that one might see in New York or Chicago. The relative equality of misfortune contributed to an egalitarian spirit of social interaction that would carry over into the next century, and

Col. Eli Lilly, 1890-94

Col. Eli Lilly was founder and first president of the Commercial Club.

The Indianapolis Board of Trade merged with the Commercial Club and four other organizations to become the Indianapolis Chamber of Commerce in 1912.

Wagon loads of herbs are delivered to Eli Lilly and Company for drug manufacturing as pictured in this scene, circa 1910.

the extent of the misfortune contributed to a conservatism about enterprise and investment that was equally long lived. Little wonder that the Board of Trade was slow to respond to the returning prosperity of the 1880s.

Fortune and Lilly Offer a New Approach

A new approach to commercial expansion and community activism was needed. In January 1890 a young writer for *The Indianapolis News*, William Fortune, wrote a series of editorials promoting the idea of a new kind of civic organization that would bring the business and professional leadership of the city together to promote economic growth and to address the city's urgent physical needs. Soon a flurry of letters to the editor appeared supporting such a plan of work and urging the formation of such an organization. Significantly for the plan's success, it received the support of one of the city's most prominent and capable businessmen, Col. Eli Lilly.

Eli Lilly was a critical factor in the character and success of the emerging city of Indianapolis, an "invaluable man." His vision, energy, and skill assured the success of many ventures. He was a native of Baltimore, Maryland, who had come west in the middle years of the century. Starting as a store clerk in Greencastle and then in Lafayette, Indiana, he had built a successful career in the emerging drug industry. He took time out to serve with distinction in the Civil War as an officer in the Union army; he commanded one of the best regarded artillery batteries in the western theater and rose to the rank of colonel. After a troubling year running a southern plantation, he returned to the drug industry, opening his own store and moving in to manufacture about the time he settled permanently in Indianapolis in 1873. For three years he had a partnership with Dr. John F. Johnston. In 1876 Lilly chose to go on his own, opening the business which became Eli Lilly and Company.

Lilly came to the industry when it was deeply divided between two groups. One consisted of the manufacturers of so-called "patent" medicines, often with an alcohol or opium base, who marketed their products chiefly as painkillers. The other group represented the manufacturers of "ethical" drugs, normally provided in response to prescriptions from medical practitioners who were laying the base of the modern pharmaceutical industry. The Colonel, as he was often called, was a firm champion of the latter group. He contributed to its ultimate success through imaginative manufacturing processes and the solid management practices of his own company.

Lilly also proved to be a man of strong personal convictions regarding the responsibilities of industrialists toward their communities. An adherent to the concept of the stewardship of wealth, he believed it appropriate to use a portion of his income to improve the city where he resided. He was a frequent contributor to charity and an active churchman who lent his name to a variety of civic improvement proposals and projects.

From small beginnings in 1876, Eli Lilly and Company grew to be a leader in the pharmaceutical industry by 1890.

The Commercial Club of Indianapolis had several forerunners:

1853-1854
   Original Indianapolis Board of Trade

1857-1870
   Reorganized Indianapolis Board of Trade

1864-1870
   Original Indianapolis Chamber of Commerce

1868-1870
   Indianapolis Merchants & Manufacturers Association

1870-onward
   Chamber of Commerce & Merchants & Manufacturers Association merge into an enlarged Board of Trade

1873
   Board of Trade creates a subsidiary company, the Indianapolis Chamber of Commerce, to erect a Board of Trade Building (sometimes called the Chamber of Commerce Building) at Maryland Street and Capitol Avenue

1890
   Commercial Club of Indianapolis organized

A plaque dedicated to Colonel Lilly was unveiled in the lobby of the Commercial Club building at 28 South Meridian Street on June 6, 1901. It is inscribed, "First president of the Commercial Club, largely through whose efforts this building was erected and in commemoration of whose services in promoting the welfare of Indianapolis this tablet is erected by members of the Commercial Club." It now adorns the landing of the Chamber building at 320 North Meridian Street.

COLONEL ELI LILLY
—1838 — 1898—
FIRST PRESIDENT OF THE COMMERCIAL CLUB LARGELY THROUGH WHOSE EFFORTS THIS BUILDING WAS ERECTED AND IN COMMEMORATION OF WHOSE SERVICES IN PROMOTING THE WELFARE OF INDIANAPOLIS THIS TABLET IS ERECTED BY MEMBERS OF THE COMMERCIAL CLUB.

CAPITAL STOCK $250,
SHARES $10 EACH

The COMMERCIAL CLUB
INDIANAPOLIS, IND.

is the owner

Capital stock subscriptions, shares at $10 each, were purchased by early members of the Club.

Civic beautification was high on that list. Speaking in the president's annual address at the February 1892 annual meeting, he articulated a personal vision of what he felt his adopted city could become :

I see a city with sidewalks smooth and even . . . shaded by trees which may be hacked to pieces by any chance butcher, but kept in order by the city forever. . . . roadways are smooth . . . alleys kept clean . . . dust is unknown and the trash heap, store sweepings, the handbill fiend, the open garbage cart and kindred evils are unknown . . . sewerage system complete . . . water is pure . . . the sad and weary streetcar mule has made his last run long since and rapid transit is everywhere. Beautiful parks are everywhere, the steam railways elevated. . . .

Such a vision suggested that a new approach to commercial expansion and community activism was needed. Lilly began addressing his vision by recognizing that a new organization, freed from the constraints of past programs, was needed. Other common names had been taken, so his new group was to be called the Commercial Club, a name that it retained until 1912. Since new challenges often require new approaches, he envisioned a group that would encourage the kinds of growth that could survive another panic.

Scientific Commercial Growth

Specifically, Lilly and his contemporaries rejected the idea that civic promotion should take the form of "brass band" methods that attracted development on the basis of personal favoritism or chance encounter. The best methods were "scientific": the preparation of statistics and maps, the presentation of advantages in transportation and communication, the assessment of available materials and markets. Industries should be encouraged only if they had a reasonable chance of success; growth should be of the kind that could withstand the pressures of economic hard times.

Twenty-seven men responded to the resulting call for an organizational meeting and gathered at the Bates House, a prominent local hotel, in February 1890. Their names read like a roster of the city's commercial leaders. Included were Harry S. New, Worth Merritt, W. H. Eastman, Francis Halliday, Charles Fletcher, Hilton U. Brown, S. E. Rauh, Edward Brown Porter, and Granville Wright.

From the start, members of the new organization made it clear that they wanted to approach the problems in a broad, systematic, and continuing manner. Important as the street question might be, their plan was to create a comprehensive organization that could address a wide range of present and future civic needs. To reflect this strong call to public action, they named their organization "The Commercial Club of Indianapolis" at their opening meeting. They declared their purpose "to promote the prosperity and work for the general welfare of Indianapolis." This state-

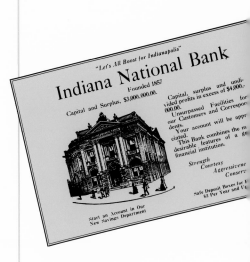

Indiana National Bank advertisement as shown in the Indianapolis Chamber magazine, *Activities,* January 1922. INB was a founding member of the Commercial Club.

Promotion of local business at the turn of the century took many forms. In May 1901 the president of the Indianapolis local of the Cigar Makers' Union approached the Commercial Club to ask for help promoting "greater consumption of Indianapolis made cigars." Unable to "describe any efficient method of complying," the Club board did the next best thing. It required that only locally made cigars be purchased for future monthly Club "smokers."

The Commercial Club Building, located on South Meridian Street at Pearl Street from 1894 to 1926, was known for its "speedy" elevators.

ment they soon refined to "promotion of the commercial and manufacturing interests and the general welfare of the city of Indianapolis, Marion County, Indiana and vicinity." Lilly was elected the Club's first president.

Within days the membership had doubled and eventually numbered eighty-one charter members. Each joined as an individual, rather than as a business or professional firm. (The organization moved to corporate memberships in the 1930s.) Together the membership of 1890 represented many of the key ventures in the city, including *The Indianapolis News,* Indiana National Bank, Kiefer-Stewart Company, the Indianapolis Board of Trade, Van Camp Hardware and Iron Company, and, of course, Eli Lilly and Company.

Next to Lilly, the key figure in the Commercial Club's early development was William Fortune. A native Hoosier, born in Boonville in 1863, Fortune had entered journalism as a printer's apprentice at age thirteen and had become a reporter for *The Indianapolis Journal* at age nineteen. There he proved to be a skilled political correspondent. His investigative reports once resulted in an attempt to expel him from the press gallery—an attempt defeated only by the support of the lieutenant governor after a tie vote in the Senate. His coverage of Benjamin Harrison's 1888 presidential campaign won him national recognition, while his energy, enthusiasm, and new ideas were winning him the reputation of a man who was able to get things done, a man who tried new ideas. He was a natural choice to be the Club's first secretary, a post he would hold for many years.

A Warm Welcome—A New Building

The charter members sought to put the Club on a sound financial footing. They created a joint stock corporation capitalized at $250,000, divided into 25,000 shares valued at $10 each. Colonel Lilly made the first subscription for $2,000; William Burford of Burford Printing, the second for $1,000. Subscribers were invited to purchase their stock in twenty monthly installments, each equal to 5 percent of the purchase price. The capital was not to be used for the routine expenses of the Club, but rather invested to support both the stockholders and the Club. Each stockholder, regardless of the size of his holdings, was entitled to one vote at the annual meeting each February, when the fifteen directors of the corporation were elected to staggered, two-year terms.

The local press was quick to welcome the new group. *The Indianapolis News* saw it as a useful contribution to a city, "presenting in every avenue those evidences of a wealth and industry that are to be found only in cities whose prosperity is assured, and whose increase in that way a constant factor." The Club, *The News* noted, would perform "a kind of work the Board of Trade is not prepared to do without enlarging its scope. . . . In the Board's present form . . . there is no provision for giving attention to general interests in the very important way now known as 'booming.'"

The *Sun* Publishing Company was even blunter: "The *Sun* declares for

William Fortune, 1897 and 1917-18
Fortune was a reporter for *The Indianapolis News* and an early promoter and secretary of the Commercial Club. C. D. Alexander, board chair of the Chamber at the time of the group's fiftieth anniversary in 1940, summarized the contributions of Fortune this way:

Fifty years ago the belief was widely held in Indianapolis that this city had no future. Many businessmen believed the city was gradually losing ground—that progress was impossible. Impatient with this defeatist attitude, a young man went to his employer on *The Indianapolis News* and asked permission to write a series of editorials urging that an organization be formed through which citizens might cooperate to work for the development of the city. Business leaders fanned the spark which he kindled into a flame . . . That man was William Fortune, who was the first secretary of the Commercial Club of Indianapolis . . .

Only the Club's cornerstone remained when the Indianapolis Chamber moved to new headquarters in 1927. The earlier building was dubbed "1891." Designed by architects, Messrs. Vonnegut & Bohn of Indianapolis, it was selected above four other designs.

View of the unpaved West Street
from Washington Street, 1896.
Street repair remained at the top
of the Club's agenda through the
1890s.

the Club; and the consequent substantial Indianapolis boom. It has always declared for anything and everything that would bring a dollar or a resident to the city."

Almost immediately the Club decided to follow the example of the Board of Trade and erect a building, both to provide a good investment income and to reflect a sense of permanence and credibility in the city. Prof. William R. Ware of Columbia College of New York was retained as a consultant by the Club to supervise a design competition that eventually produced five finalists, titled *Hoosier, Cornucopia, Levant, Theta,* and *1891.*

The eventual winner, *1891,* was the creation of a local architectural firm, Vonnegut and Bohn. The design called for an eight-story building on South Meridian Street. It was built in 1893 and 1894 and at once became one of the showpieces of the city. Visitors were whisked in high speed elevators to a top floor restaurant with an excellent view of the city, including the War Memorial then emerging on the Circle. The Club itself took quarters on the seventh floor, while renting offices to tenants who would abide by such rules as no peddlers, no bootblacks, no animals, no bicycles in the halls, and no rug shaking out of windows.

A Bold Civic Agenda

Hand in hand with its own organizational initiatives, the Commercial Club addressed itself to civic needs. Not surprisingly, the first major agenda item was the street question. Just forty days after its founding, the Club gained national attention by holding "The Street Paving Exposition of Indianapolis."

Invitations were sent to the major contractors and manufacturers bidding for municipal paving contracts. Fifty-five exhibitors came to the city in the spring of 1890 with samples, drawings, and examples of construction methods. Present as well were representatives of forty cities and towns, including Omaha, Lexington, and Hartford, to review the relative merits, costs, and cleaning properties of brick, clay, crushed stone, and Indiana limestone blocks. Displays were set out on three-foot-wide tables; the exhibition stretched 350 feet. Crowds were heavy at each of the three public buildings to which the exhibition eventually moved. In a pointed dig at the City Council, the exhibits were contrasted with the city's past use of Vulcanite, a patented asbestos derivative that had proved so soft in the summer heat of 1889 that the Club's 1891 *Annual Report* noted that "a loaded team will sink into [it] if allowed to stand any length of time."

The exposition greatly enhanced the credibility of the new group—for its efficiency in implementing its plans, for its 500 delegates and 12,000 attendees, and for the attention it attracted to the city. But it also highlighted a major consideration of the Club's early years: its relationship with local government.

D. P. Erwin, 1895-96
David M. Parry, 1898

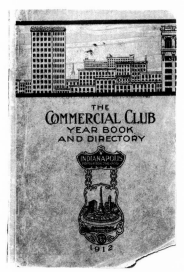

In an effort to promote commerce among its members, the Commercial Club began publishing and marketing a business directory as early as 1912.

The early Commercial Club logo was used on many of the Club's publications.

The Club was primary sponsor of the 1893 Grand Army of the Republic Encampment, whose centerpiece, the U.S. ship *Kearsarge,* famous for sinking the Confederate raider *Alabama,* was reassembled on the State House lawn.

At its founding meeting the Club had specifically rejected local political involvement, just as most of its founding members had avoided local public office. Yet the issues before the group touched closely upon the public sector and impelled them to define their relationship to city government. The answer, a partnership in which the Commercial Club would play the role of interested adviser, soon followed.

This partnership became apparent when the Club took a leading role in promoting revision of the Indianapolis city charter. Many advocates of reform were frustrated or troubled by a structure that gave the mayor little power beyond chairing the council and the police court, and thus provided no focus for leadership on concerns (such as street paving) that were of interest to the Club. In March 1890 a study committee was formed jointly by the Commercial Club and the Board of Trade to review the alternative forms of city government in America, particularly those of such reform-minded locales as Brooklyn, and to recommend changes to be presented in the 1891 session of the Indiana General Assembly.

The task force looked at, and debated, various alternatives before recommending a new city charter that would separate the three branches of government and provide a mayor so strong he would even have the power to revoke saloon licenses. Approved by the parent bodies in the fall, the proposal was then taken to the state legislature, where the Club and its supporters mounted a model lobbying effort. Support was given to favorable legislators as they ran for leadership posts, pressure was put upon apprehensive public utilities to stay out of the debate, arguments were mustered to every objection (including the fear that party patronage might be lost), and passage was won in March of 1891. The Commercial Club's credibility was enhanced accordingly.

In the years that followed, the Club worked with city government for many common objectives. Twenty volunteer Club members joined public officials in conducting the lagging property tax assessment of 1891. Plans for a new city jail were jointly reviewed. A Club-sponsored referendum was held to promote new taxes for street improvement (although the vote was a disappointing 434 yes and 464 no). Most important, the Commercial Club pushed for the creation of a city park commission that would be specifically charged to develop a system of public parks and green spaces along Pleasant Run, Fall Creek, and White River and to maintain the spaces surrounding such public buildings as the U. S. Arsenal adjoining Woodruff Place.

A Civic Greeting

The Commercial Club also took the lead in encouraging visitors to come to the city, particularly for conferences and conventions. The 1890s saw a remarkable number of voluntary associations form and re-form, offering a fertile field to the community able to host their regional and national conventions and reunions. Given its location as a major Ameri-

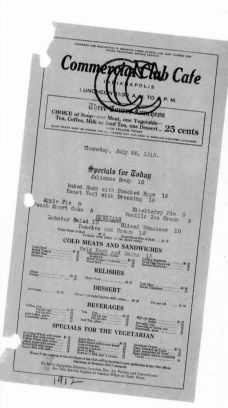

According to local legend, the Club's cafe had the "best meal in town," including roast veal with dressing and blackberry pie for only twenty cents.

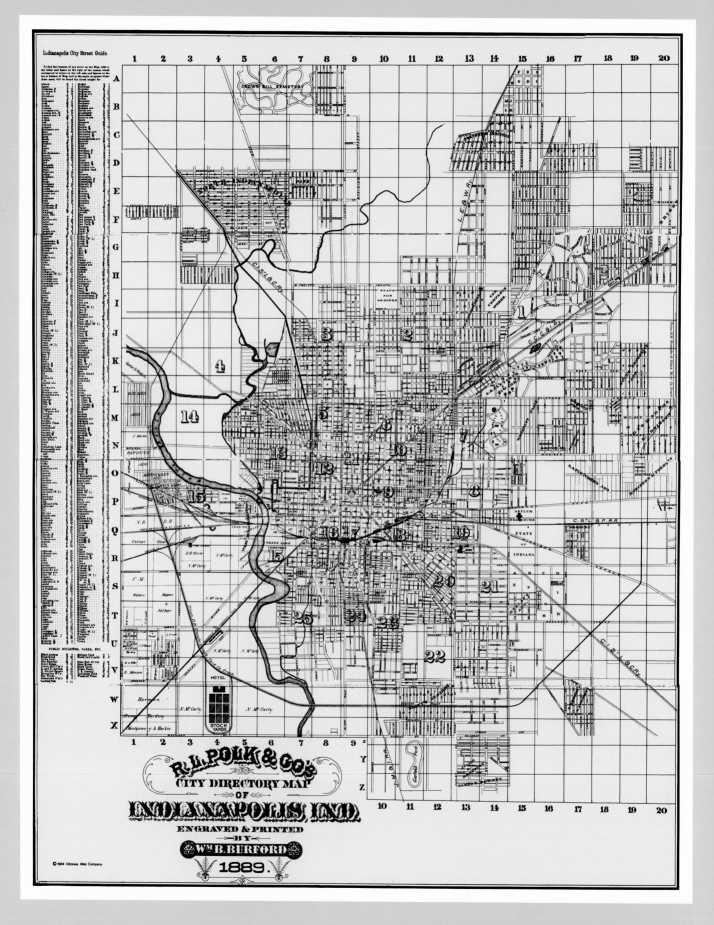

R.L. POLK & CO's
CITY DIRECTORY MAP
OF
INDIANAPOLIS, IND.
ENGRAVED & PRINTED
BY
Wm. B. BURFORD
1889.

© 1984 Odyssey Map Company

can railroad center, Indianapolis was well suited to assume the role—and the Club was clearly interested. Some of its activities were minor, such as providing streetcar passes to the members of the Supreme Grove of the United Ancient Order of Druids in 1900. Others involved more effort.

The most important of these was the invitation to the Grand Army of the Republic (GAR) to hold its Twenty-seventh National Encampment in Indianapolis in 1893. This gathering of veterans of the Union army eventually involved nearly 3,000 local citizens, organized into thirty committees, who were responsible for planning and raising funds for the event. Attended by about 250,000 people, including families and visitors, it was the largest gathering yet held in the city—and one of the few encampments to end up in the black. As chairman of the event, Colonel Lilly took pride in bringing the event in under cost, although a legal challenge to his expenses took five years to be resolved in his favor in the courts.

Publicized activities were essential to the growth of the early Club. But they were only a part of its achievement, much of which took the quiet form of the collection and dissemination of information about the city.

Relief Initiatives

The Club also showed a special concern for citizen relief after another major depression struck. In the winter of 1893 the Club's Relief Committee sought to coordinate efforts to identify the unemployed and to find work for them with both public agencies and private employers. A special food and fuel bank was established, its initial stocks paid for by membership subscriptions and available at discounted prices to men with proof they had performed useful work. Credit was extended to public works employees whom the city could not pay at the time. Persons who could not work were referred to charitable agencies. Nearly 1,500 men were referred to jobs the committee located; nearly 1,900 workers (1,117 white, 772 black) received food or coal credits. The operations, praised by one national commentator as a triumph of scientific management, showed the ability of the Club to adapt its ideas to new settings and challenges.

A Sound Foundation

Not every project of the early Commercial Club met with success. Plans for a world's fair failed to receive the necessary funding, proposals to woo the Cincinnati baseball club to Indianapolis came to naught, and requests to the steam railroads to elevate their tracks at grade crossings met with repeated refusals. But balanced against these setbacks was a bold record of achievement that set the pattern for future activity. The emphasis upon a sound financial base, upon "scientific" promotion of the city, upon effective management practices, upon nonpartisan cooperation with government, and upon the beautification of the city all suggested that the direction of the Club was established early. Lilly, Fortune, and their contemporaries had done a solid job of laying the foundation for the future.

Under the direction of Colonel Lilly, the Chamber organized Indianapolis' first major convention, the Grand Army of the Republic Twenty-seventh National Encampment, which brought in more than 250,000 union army veterans and other visitors to the city in 1893.

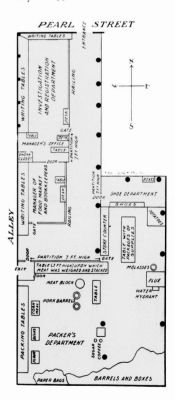

The Commercial Club Relief Committee food market, operated from the Club offices, served many hard-pressed people in the winter of 1893.

The Virginia Avenue viaduct dedication, circa 1890, was part of a city-wide track elevation project lifting rail lines above streets.

It's hard to tell who had the right-of-way in this 1906 scene at the Washington Street and Illinois Street intersection.

Chapter 2

Serving The Industrial City

The Commercial Club that entered the twentieth century described itself in its 1904 annual membership mailing as a "live, wide-awake civic and commercial organization," whose policy was to "get results and let the credit take care of itself." Results, for many Indianapolis citizens, meant responses to powerful forces of change and a new American spirit of urban reform—a spirit that demanded more efficient public services, more attention to the social and economic needs of recent immigrants and other disadvantaged groups, and more participation by community leaders in the public life of the city. Termed "progressivism" by many national political figures, the urban reform movement took differing forms in different cities, while touching nearly all.

The Commercial Club Becomes the Chamber of Commerce

The Commercial Club had already shown its effective support of urban improvement in the 1890s, particularly in successful involvement in street resurfacing, in relief work during the Panic of 1893, and in advocacy of a new city charter. By the early twentieth century the remaining challenges—particularly such complex and intractable problems as track elevation and public health—convinced Club leaders of the need for a broader base of support. They also recognized that an expanded organization could, in turn, act on an ever wider range of business and civic challenges.

The Commercial Club accordingly approached other active business organizations in Indianapolis and proposed a merger. Five groups responded favorably: the Adscript Club, the Freight Bureau, the Indianapolis Trade Association, the Manufacturers Association, and the Merchants Association. The merger united voices of the primary business activities of the Hoosier capital city: publishing, shipping, wholesaling, manufacturing, and retailing. The new organization was formally established on December 17, 1912. It took the name it retains to this day, the Indianapolis Chamber of Commerce.

The Commercial Club was the most important partner in the merger. The Club's civic agenda became the Chamber's agenda, and preexisting Club programs continued uninterrupted after the merger. Only two main changes were apparent after 1912. First, the merger brought together an increased number of active members and concerned citizens. Second, it encouraged the new Chamber to speak more frequently

John M. Spann, 1901
Frank E. Gavin, 1902-03

John W. Kern, 1904
Alfred F. Potts, 1905

The modern **Indianapolis Chamber of Commerce** was formed in 1912 from a merger of the **Commercial Club of Indianapolis** with:
• the **Adscript Club**
• the **Freight Bureau**
• the **Indianapolis Trade Association**
• the **Manufacturers Association**
• the **Merchants Association**

Top Left: Track elevation and clean air were two concerns that convinced the Commercial Club and five other business organizations to unite as the Indianapolis Chamber of Commerce in 1912.

Top Right: Track removal along the rising Pennsylvania Railroad viaduct, May 16, 1919. Track elevation was completed in the Mile Square area when the last grade crossing was removed three years later.

Bottom: Natural gas depletion gave rise to coal burning businesses by the turn of the century, increasing the Indianapolis Chamber's concern for clean air.

and forcefully on avowedly business topics such as freight rates and industrial promotion.

Continuing Concerns: Public Safety and Air Quality

Improved public safety was one example of a civic concern that was equally important both before and after the 1912 merger. In 1901 the Commercial Club noted the rapid rise in the use of coal as a heating fuel in the city. The change was the result of the rapid depletion of the natural gas fields to the north of Marion County, which led to problems of supply, pressure, and cost. Yet growing dependence upon coal soon produced the black (soot-covered) snows of winter and brought a new danger of fire from improperly installed or tended furnaces and flues.

The Club soon became interested in smoke abatement. An educational campaign showed how to install and fire furnaces safely and spoke up for alternatives to coal usage. A new citizen-controlled company, ultimately named Citizens Gas, that would provide cheap, clean, and dependable sources of natural gas, was supported as an alternative to greater coal dependence.

Smoke abatement soon led to fire safety concerns. Beyond questions of esthetics, the safety campaign reflected concern over the rapidly rising costs of fire insurance in the city. Between 1905 and 1910 the safety program became a major Club activity. The group campaigned for more fire equipment, better training of firemen, and new pumping facilities to provide better water pressure to the fire hydrants. With this came a new emphasis upon revising and tightening the building codes to help reduce the threat of fire in both old and new structures. Coal furnaces came in for special attention, along with construction materials, hazardous chemicals, and flammable wastes.

Alarmed by fireworks injuries to the young, the Club next adopted a "safe and sane" stance toward the Fourth of July in 1909. It also lobbied for restrictions on the sale of dangerous fireworks to minors. In subsequent years the campaign was accompanied by public parades, one of which numbered over forty wagons.

Campaigns by the new Chamber to attract new industry were conducted with similar attention to the need for safety in the workplace, culminating in the "Safety First" campaign in 1914. Proponents were quick to tie this safety campaign to the dangers posed to pedestrians by railroad and interurban grade crossings, effectively linking the campaign to the long-standing call for track elevation.

Modern Public Health

Along with public safety came concern for public health. The decade between 1900 and 1910 was a watershed period in America. Both medical and public figures enthusiastically adopted one new measure after another to combat epidemic disease, curb infant mortality, and improve

Local manufacturers were quick to capitalize on the public's irritation with "soot-covered winters." The product "Carbonoid" was advertised as "a granulated carbon which, when placed directly on a red hot bed of coals, removes and consumes all soot in furnaces, ranges, boiler flues, chimneys or pipes . . . and saves you money!"

The Engine House No. 30 "Sprinkling Party." The Commercial Club, and later the Indianapolis Chamber, worked with local fire departments to promote better training and equipment for firemen, leading to a full-blown "Safety First" campaign in 1914.

31

Top: Public health was a vital issue in the early twentieth century. This horse-drawn smallpox ambulance was used by City Hospital from 1905 to 1908.

Bottom: The Commercial Club became a sponsor of the new Indiana Association for the Prevention of Tuberculosis in 1907. The Boy Scouts were among the most vocal proponents for clean city streets.

the quality of personal health. A series of epidemics, including a 1901 typhoid scare and the later 1919 influenza outbreak, assured an attentive public response.

As early as 1901 the Commercial Club advocated a sanitary sewer system to replace undrained private vaults. The Club also called for a halt to street dumping after one offender dumped a truckload of refuse on the Court House square.

In 1907 the Club became a sponsor of the new Indiana Association for the Prevention of Tuberculosis. A year later it endorsed a separate hospital (actually a separate wing of City Hospital) for contagious disease, and in 1914 endorsed a county tuberculosis hospital. Calls for a sewage treatment plant and for public comfort stations soon followed.

In 1907 a report on city social conditions drew attention to the poor quality of housing in many congested areas. It prompted the Club's support of anti-tenement legislation in the General Assembly and gave support for public baths and an expanded street cleaning program.

The new Chamber continued this emphasis when it launched its "anti-fly" campaign. This initiative was accompanied by an extensive educational effort to encourage covered trash cans, clean streets, and bring an end to keeping livestock on residential property. Using the slogan "Prevent the Fly and Swat the Fly," the Chamber hired speakers and obtained prizes from local businessmen for the youths who brought in the greatest volume of dead flies—by weight—during the campaign.

Agricultural economists were encouraged to lecture on proper nutrition for the young, and from 1915 to 1918 the Chamber conducted a "clean milk" campaign in conjunction with local dairies.

Education and Persuasion, Not Coercion

The organization's leaders walked a fine line in many of its education and awareness activities, striving to encourage public improvements without infringing on private rights in the process. As the Commercial Club's *Annual Report* of 1906 observed, "The aim of this Club is not so much to increase the number of our population as the quality of the citizenship; not so much to have a big city as to have a good one." Yet, as the 1908 *Annual Report* observed, "Vexatious questions are continually arising demanding careful judgment, so as to avoid, if possible, interference with individual liberty and rights, but so as to overcome and dispel encroachments on public welfare."

The result was a series of campaigns geared to education and persuasion rather than to coercion, with the assumption that government or private welfare activities would follow if the Commercial Club (later the Chamber) took the lead. Arthur Dunn, a Shortridge High School teacher, writing in a study commissioned by the Chamber, caught the spirit: "The work of civic instruction and the work of civic improvement . . . are but two phases of the same movement toward better communal life."

An illustration on an Indiana Board of Health postcard highlights a concern that led to the Chamber's "anti-fly" campaign in 1908.

"Prevent the Fly and Swat the Fly"

Red Cross volunteers raise money to fight tuberculosis near the steps outside the Federal Building, circa 1915.

Students at Shortridge High School, circa 1916. Support of higher salaries for teachers was among the Commercial Club's efforts to improve education in the early 1900s.

Public Welfare

These attitudes assured continued Chamber interest in public welfare. In the closely connected matter of charities, the Chamber was a constant advocate of cooperation that would most effectively manage and direct scarce resources.

The need came keenly to the fore in 1913 when the city experienced its worst natural disaster of modern times, the great White River flood. The flood plain to the west of the city center was inundated. It forced extensive evacuations, temporary resettlement, and a major clean-up effort conducted under the auspices of a committee created by the Chamber. The Chamber similarly took a leading role in advocating new levees and the other flood control measures that commenced in 1914.

Two years later saw the appearance of several bogus charities that raised money with little or no intention of providing charitable services. This prompted the Chamber to create a special committee that investigated each charity and issued cards with Chamber recommendation to those that won endorsement—anticipating the Federation of Charities that followed in 1916.

Three years later, William Fortune, then serving as Chamber president, proposed another innovative step: the creation of a nonpolitical community welfare board enabled by law to accept bequests and gifts for benefit of the city.

Partners with Government

Government activity under the new city charter also continued to attract the Club's and Chamber's attention. Most public program proposals depended upon government cooperation, a cooperation that was most apparent in continued city beautification measures. From the creation of the park system in 1897 onward, the Commercial Club was an advocate of green public spaces in Indianapolis, particularly those tied to the city's waterways. Highest priority went to the boulevards, parks, and levees along Fall Creek which began to appear in 1903. Support for bridges over White River and Fall Creek and for electric lighting for city streets soon followed. A 1914 "vacant lot cultivation" campaign and a 1916 "clean-up, paint-up" campaign again suggested the desire for a partnership of public and private activity.

This range of interests and emphasis upon partnership suggested the need for a membership base sufficient to support an expanding program. At its founding, the Commercial Club had set a goal of 2,500 dues-paying members, and during the 1890s it had regularly maintained a base of between 700 and 800. Much of this was a result of the work of the Club's officers, especially Fortune. It reflected the ties and linkages to the founding members or the appeal of the Club's downtown building and activi-

A street car, left abandoned in the 1913 White River flood, is a reminder of one of the city's most severe natural disasters. On May 26, after five days of heavy rains, nearly $25 million in damage was recorded in the Indianapolis area. The Chamber joined relief committees to supply food, clothing, and housing to refugees.

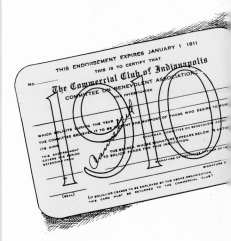

The Commercial Club's card of endorsement was issued first in 1916 to help bring an end to several bogus charities. By 1916 the Federation of Charities was established.

This witty rendering characterizing activities of the Indianapolis Chamber's membership committee appeared in *The Kidder,* a popular local magazine, in 1915.

ties. Only after 1900 were membership campaigns run on a systematic basis that involved substantial numbers of individual members.

The big change came when the Commercial Club created a membership committee charged with preparing lists of potential recruits—many of whose names were drawn from lists of businesses prepared by the Club's research committees—and then individually contacting their owners. The shift from individual to business membership combined with the new membership committee to produce substantial growth. By 1912 a committee of over 100 had produced a membership close to 1,500, who were paying dues increased to ten dollars in 1904 and to fifteen dollars in 1911.

The merger of 1912 that created the Chamber, and the vigorous activity shown in the health, safety, and flood relief campaigns, prompted one Club officer to proclaim in *The Indianapolis Star* in 1915 that "the Chamber is doing effectively what six separate organizations attempted to do in the past." Such energy was reflected in the Chamber's membership drive of 1915. It set a goal of 1,000 new members, which would essentially double its size in a single year. The campaign slogan was "Cooperation Butters More Slices of Bread Than Indifference." One participant called the drive "a workshop of extensive proportions." It made the next four years the Chamber's greatest growth period, ending with over 3,800 individual members in 1919.

Contributions to Business Growth

Such impressive growth also bore evidence of the growth of Indianapolis itself in the first two decades of the new century. The population advanced from 160,000 to 350,000 and industrial production increased from $69 million to over $300 million. As the Chamber itself later noted in its 1926 *Annual Report,* "Prior to 1900 industrial development was a thing almost unknown. Factories came and went, but little attention, in a general way, was paid to their coming or to their departure. Each manufacturer was left to shoulder his own burdens, to work out his own problems and his own salvation."

Such an analysis understated the solid foundation of Commercial Club activity in the 1890s. But it did capture the sense shared by many Chamber members after 1900 that they needed to implement changes in their approach if they were to contribute meaningfully to the expansion that they desired. As the 1926 *Annual Report* put it, "These things have not come about as matters of chance. Cities grow because they are made to grow. . . . While Indianapolis has been making these rapid strides, numerous other cities have fallen behind in comparison."

The Plan of Work

Four major steps dominated the activities of the Commercial Club and the ensuing Chamber between 1900 and 1919. These were aggressive

Walton L. Dynes, 1909
Winfield Miller, 1910

The Indianapolis Chamber's "Clean-Up, Paint-Up" campaign in 1916 led to the razing of deteriorating structures and urban eyesores.

Continuing the tradition of the Commercial Club founders, the Indianapolis Chamber issued stock to each of its members as late as 1930.

Madame C. J. Walker, a nationally
recognized leader in business and
civic affairs in the early 1900s,
posed with four distinguished men
of her time at the Indianapolis
Senate Avenue YMCA dedication in
1913. Left to right: George Knox,
Madame C. J. Walker, F. B. Ran-
som, Booker T. Washington, Alexander Manning, Dr. Joseph Ward,
R.W. Tucker, and Thomas A. Taylor.

publicity, intense railway rate negotiations, industrial site development, and vigorous solicitation of wartime contracts.

Publicity was the earliest and the most sustained. R. Webb Sparks, a later director of promotion, recalled in a 1926 memoir prepared for the dedicatory program of the new Chamber building, "Publicity in 1892 was as different from publicity in 1926 as was the horseless carriage of 1894 from the luxurious limousine of today. . . . For the first eight or ten years the publicity efforts of the old Commercial Club were rather desultory in nature, but effective, nevertheless. There were groups charged with the responsibility of promoting publicity, but there was no paid publicity man, as the organization depended upon the reporters of the daily papers to look after the general publicity."

The shift began in 1904 when the Press Committee directed the Club's attention to printed promotional materials. They first prepared a short leaflet and a longer booklet attesting to the advantages of Indianapolis as a residential and business city—printing and distributing 300,000 of the former and 10,000 of the latter. Then in 1907-08 the Club prepared a special *Souvenir Book* with thirteen pages of reading and 160 halftone views of Indianapolis. Six thousand copies were provided free to local residents and potential investors. This was followed in 1908 with a four-page leaflet, *Facts about Indianapolis,* which in various revisions became the standard mailing of the Chamber after 1912.

On at least one occasion, the new Chamber followed these mailings with a railroad excursion to promote the same ideas. Alarmed by aggressive campaigns by Chicago and Cincinnati jobbers in 1913, the group organized a "Know Your City" campaign that sent 3,000 people on an industrial voyage of discovery around the Belt Railroad that was designed to alert residents to the industrial strengths of the city.

Other publicity innovations followed. In 1909 the Club developed a special city badge, depicting the Monument surrounded by a stylized Belt Railway. On Indianapolis Day, December 10, 1909, they published 10,000 copies of a new magazine, *Forward.* The Chamber hired a full-time publicity man in 1917 and made a new magazine, *Heart O' Trade,* his first project. Although the underlying assumption of the early years—scientific promotion supported by careful statistical research—was unchanged, the manner of presentation was clearly moving rapidly into the age of advertising.

The Railway Rate Question

The second major challenge, railway rate improvements, reflected the special situation of the city. Unlike many major urban centers that are located on navigable water, Indianapolis has always recognized that its economic vitality is dependent upon man-made means of transportation. In the late nineteenth and early twentieth centuries, that meant the steam railways.

Cassius C. Hadley, 1911
Frank M. McAllister, 1912

The Chamber dedicated a new building at 320 North Meridian Street in 1926.

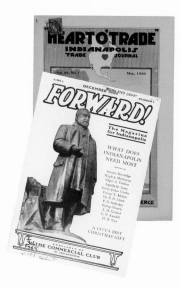

The Commercial Club gave rise to public promotion with the publication of its first magazine, *Forward!,* in 1909, and the journal, *Heart O' Trade,* in 1917.

The Fletcher Bank on Massachusetts Avenue advertises Mars Hill
industrial and suburban tracts
southwest of Indianapolis, circa
1912. The Indianapolis Chamber
vigorously worked for the promotion and sale of the Mars Hill lots.

City maps of that era reveal a pattern of business intimately tied to the rail lines. Downtown, near the 1888 Union Station, was a large warehouse district. Nearby, tied to the Belt Railway, were the Stockyards and other agricultural processing firms, of which Kingan and Company was probably the best known. Along the other lines, such as those extending up Massachusetts Avenue, were a variety of manufacturing firms, many of which were suppliers to the railways themselves.

This situation tied any substantial economic growth, and even the success of existing businesses, to the shipping charges on those railways. In 1906 those rates became the subject of federal legislation under the Hepburn Act, which sought to eliminate unfair rate discrimination against certain shippers or certain communities. Convinced that the enforcement of the Act would benefit Indianapolis shippers, the Commercial Club promptly created a Freight Bureau. According to the 1926 *Annual Report*, the Freight Bureau was created to "apply these principles to the particular situation here so that our shipping may be fully protected . . . [and because] . . . the conclusion is inescapable that the interests of shippers could not have been properly protected except through the constant efforts of such an agency."

The period 1906 to 1917 became an era of intense negotiation in front of the Interstate Commerce Commission. The Freight Bureau, and its successor under the Chamber, the Traffic Division, repeatedly protested against existing or proposed rates on the railroads. Rare periods of cooperation, generally tied to the carriers' fear of greater federal intervention, highlighted the adversarial relationship that prevailed and that helped to define the Chamber's membership and direction of activity. Problems of freight charges did not disappear in 1917, but they were then absorbed into the larger concern involving the Chamber in World War I efforts.

Industrial Site Promotion

Attempts to take advantage of its extensive railroad network also contributed to the third major activity of the Chamber, industrial site promotion. Arguing in its minute book that "the welfare of Indianapolis at this time demands an enlargement of its industrial activity," the group in 1912 took over the promotion of the Mars Hill Enterprise southwest of the city. Two earlier groups had failed in their efforts to promote the area as an "industrial suburb," either by providing inexpensive industrial sites or by attracting home builders to the 2,000 residential lots that were designed to provide worker housing.

Determined, as its minute book noted, to "present Mars Hill industrial suburb to Indianapolis as a birthday present," the Chamber took over promotional activity. The Chamber was convinced that the development of the residential area would provide a pool of workers that in turn would attract industry, and applied its proven techniques of membership recruitment to land sales. Offering the lots for $400 each, $100 of which

Musical Programme
Commercial Club Annual Dinner
November 15, 1912

"OUR COMMERCIAL CLUB"
(Tune of "Turkey in the Straw")
Lyric by Bergeh W. Plummer
I.
Nifty Josie Reagan's an exclusive old bird
Since he joined our Commercial Club—oh! my word!
He deals in "baubles" that would make a greenhorn weep,
But it's nothing but jewelry, and it's jewelry cheap.

CHORUS
Eddie Gauspohl's a merry old soul,
Fiddler at heart, but it ain't his goal;
His trunks are punk, but we'll all have to swear
That he dotes on chicken dinners at our Indianny Fair!

II.
Doctor Henry Jameson's a very knowing "Med.,"
And there's lots of thoughtful microbes rambling through his brainy head;
But there's something peeved the Doctor and it made him fret and fidge
Til' he floated that Cap-itol Avenue Bridge!

CHORUS
Oscar L. Pond is an LL. D.,
But Ponds ain't as deep as the deep blue sea.
Whether Ponds or puddles, he's far from a dub
So long as he's Vice President of our Commercial Club.

III.
Now our old friend Freddie Hoke is a mighty serious joke,
And he'd like to chaw terbacker, but his wifie makes him smoke;
He's a very high flyer, but he's not a highball,
And the only thing that Fred can say is "Wilson—that's all!"

CHORUS
Master Huey, the youngest of the clan,
Can outwalk our President, that Paper man;
And our J. Geo. Mueller, tho' a high-steppin' hoss,
Cannot smell so awful dopey if he smokes a "Flor-de-Moss."

IV.
Now our little Bob McClure is no ordinary jay;
It's no sign that he's insane 'cause he likes Broadway;
He's a little "Bugs" on Dixie and he likes his pictures took,
But I reckon at that he's a long ways from a crook.

CHORUS
Franklin Vonnegut, that Hardware man,
Ain't a "bone-head" and no "also-ran;"
And there's not a lad among us we can call a "dub;"
So here's a darn good health to our own Commercial Club!

The duties of office in the Commercial Club included attending the annual November dinner, perhaps to be serenaded as the 1912 officers were. "Our Commercial Club" should be sung to the tune of "Turkey in the Straw."

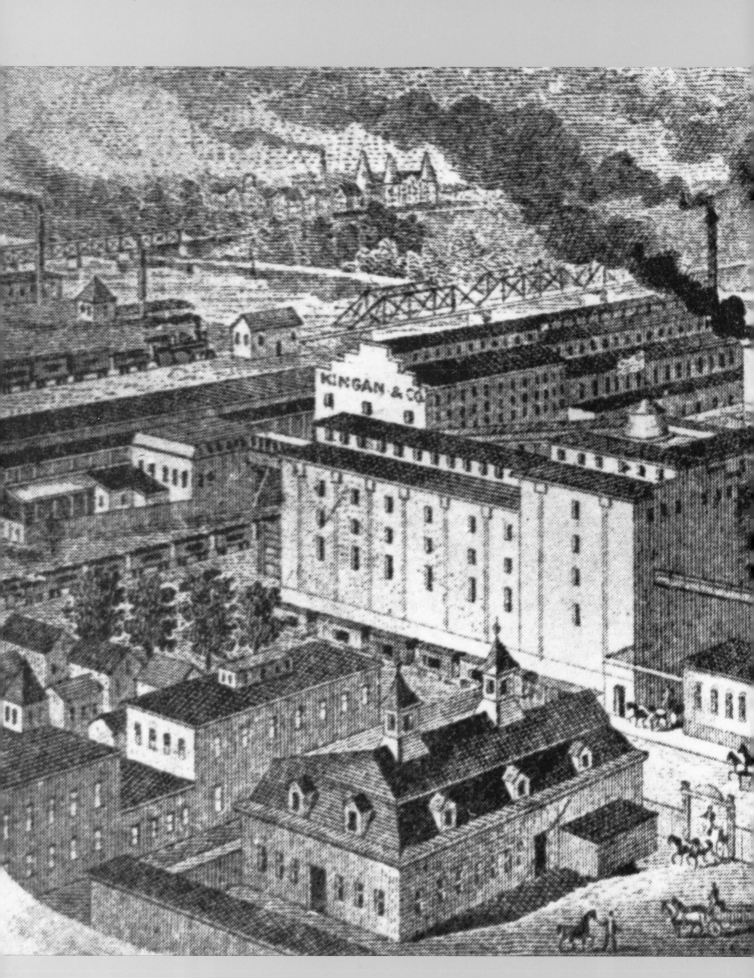

The White River, with its ready supply of water, was the first industrial area of Indianapolis. Flour millers, meat packers, and other food processors were particularly attracted to Indianapolis at the center of the rich farming area of central Indiana, Kingan and Company, originally of Belfast, Ireland, was well known for its refrigerated system of pork packing. The center of this bustling industrial sector, Kingan made Indianapolis fifth in meat packing in the nation by 1919.

Top: Who could guess what Polk's Best is?

Bottom: The Belt Railroad and Stockyards Company was an important part of the early industrial belt tied to the city's railway system.

represented stock in the Greater Indianapolis Industrial Association that would share in the industrial land sales, the Chamber sent teams of salesmen into the city. Mayor Lew Shank and other public officials joined in the campaign, which absorbed virtually all the energy of the Chamber for several months before the goal was reached.

Important as each of these local efforts was, it would be a mistake to see the Chamber as a purely local organization. The minute books of the era reveal a very active interest in issues involving the city in national and world affairs. Commercial Club and Chamber discussions regularly contained notes on such topics as the best location of a Central American canal, visits of Chinese dignitaries, and participation in international trade fairs. A severe southern depression in 1916 produced support for a "Buy a Bale of Cotton" campaign, while discussions of educational reforms in the public schools frequently included questions of language instruction for recent immigrants.

Patriotism and War

Concern for active federal involvement in community growth was a part of this interest. Just as the Chamber had taken the lead in advocating the new Federal Building at Meridian and Ohio in the 1890s, it campaigned for the establishment and then the expansion of a military post—ultimately named Fort Benjamin Harrison—near the city.

Interest in national affairs was normally expressed in the language of patriotism common to the era, particularly after the campaign for a "safe and sane" Fourth of July became a major event on the group's calendar. Such patriotic expressions became linked to economic policy in 1913 when a series of labor disturbances triggered the concern that outside organizers might disrupt the good relationships between business and labor that had prevailed for the early years of the century.

The outbreak of war in Europe in 1914 quickly caused these varied themes to be merged into an interest in civilian awareness, military training, and economic activity that is usually called the "preparedness movement." In Indianapolis the movement took the form of expanded patriotic celebrations, support for National Guard recruitment, and discussions of possible war contracts with the belligerent powers. Local motion picture theaters were asked to show only patriotic films on the Fourth of July.

In 1917 the actual entry of the United States into combat, and the subsequent adoption of wartime mobilization, moved these interests to center stage. In July of that year the Chamber appointed B. A. Worthington to head a special committee to investigate the opportunities for manufacturers, including the possible addition of new plants. A special Awakening Fund was established to provide funds to attract and support new businesses that might help to expand or "awaken" the local economy. In the fall a new War Contract Bureau was established under Chamber auspices.

In both 1914 and 1918 the Indianapolis advertisers won the prestigious Baltimore Truth Trophy of the Associated Advertising Clubs of the World for its work in fostering truth-in-advertising. Delighted, the Chamber hired a local artisan to commemorate the event by painting the word "truth" on each street lamp globe in the Mile Square. Unfortunately, as the Chamber's monthly bulletin, *Activities,* noted, "the word 'truth' on the globes was supposed to have been painted with a water color that would disappear with the first rain, but the sign painter instead used indelible black, which will stay on the globes until they are all broken."

At least, the Chamber sighed, it was "evidence of the integrity of Indianapolis retailers."

Top: The Commercial Club helped form the War Chest, precursor of today's United Way, to benefit World War I efforts and the local community.

Bottom: Support for World War I grew slowly in Indianapolis, but patriotism ran high in 1917 as citizens rallied around the flag on the westside of the city.

The new Bureau was initially a liaison office designed to put local manufacturers in touch with government agencies. Operating from offices in both Washington and Indianapolis, it was charged to notify local manufacturers of contracts about to be let, to put businessmen in contact with the actual government officials responsible for specifications, and to publicize contracts awarded to Indianapolis firms. From there it was a short step to actively lobbying for contracts, placing local leaders in contact with government officials, and actually placing bids for local firms.

Eventually dubbed the "Indianapolis Plan," the project achieved both local and national praise. A number of other cities quickly copied the approach, which received praise from government officials for speeding the process of procurement and which was hailed in a local paper as "of substantial benefit in putting Indiana on the map as a great manufacturing state through persistent presentation of its facilities to purchasing heads in Washington, many of whom have not hitherto been well informed about manufacturing resources west of the Atlantic seaboard."

The Chamber also took the lead in showing local support for the war. In 1918 it entered into a contract with the War Department to house, feed, and instruct 13,000 soldiers as auto mechanics, drivers, and carpenters. The entire Metropole Hotel at Capitol and Ohio was leased. There the Chamber trained 130 instructors who were drawn from local factories and garages and who were capable of instructing up to 2,500 men at a time. The group then tested its system with 500 drafted men from Kentucky. It was soon running the largest vocational training detachment in the United States under a single management. Accomplished on time and under budget, it was later commended as "probably the most efficiently operated detachment in the whole country."

The early years of the twentieth century, in short, had represented a substantial expansion of the design of the founders of 1890. Joined to its original interest were a greatly increased membership, many drawn from the new partners of the 1912 merger, who had substantially advanced the concept of "scientific" support for the city's commercial base. The Chamber was posed to respond to the next great era in Indianapolis history, the age of light industry.

Col. Russell B. Harrison penned a tribute to his father, President Benjamin Harrison, and to the military base that bears his name, in a souvenir book published in 1917. Benjamin Harrison, guest of honor at an annual meeting of the Commercial Club at the turn of the century, characterized Indianapolis in words that stand forever as a motto of its civic pride—"No Mean City." Fort Benjamin Harrison itself has long been a source of civic pride.

Artists help raise funds for a Liberty Bond Drive during World War I by practicing their crafts for public display on Monument Circle.

Airplanes circle overhead as soldiers march along flower-strewn Meridian Street to a victory arch erected at the south entry of Monument Circle on Welcome Home Day, Sept. 7, 1919.

The Chamber boasted Indian-apolis as "the rising star of the industrial world" in aggressive economic development efforts as early as 1920. This intricate illustration, from an elaborately produced brochure to a nationwide audience, featured the center of a changing Indianapolis. Its cover posed the question "Somewhere In America There Is An Economic Point?"

A view of Market Street looking southeast, 1922, illustrates the commercial vitality of the early 1920s. Chamber-supported improvements to rural county roads made the Indianapolis market more accessible to farmers outside the city.

Chapter 3

A Golden Age

The Indianapolis Chamber in the 1920s shared in a golden age of American chambers of commerce. It was a decade in which their activities were particularly effective, and their messages of civic growth and improvement enjoyed especially wide support and respect. Such success reflected the widespread prosperity of a decade when real wages and living standards rose for most urban families. It also reflected the excellent leadership of the proud Hoosier organization, a leadership that was both confident and concerned about the future.

Community Confidence and Pride

Local pride was never in question. Meredith Nicholson, local author and editor, captured its spirit when he noted in the Chamber's 1920 *Activities,* "The continuing charm of Indianapolis lies in the sturdy Americanism and broad democracy of its founders. A certain folksiness and neighborliness of pioneer life retained is the secret of the real Indianapolis atmosphere."

Local confidence was also strong. As one Chamber publication declared in 1926, "If it is industrial expansion that is fundamental to the growth of a city, then Indianapolis will continue to grow. Twenty-six years of persistent effort have laid the foundations for more than doubling the population. Thirty years more, or the year 1960, will yield a population of 1,000,000 at the present rate. With the application of new and intensified co-operative effort, this goal will be reached much sooner."

H. L. Dithmer, Chamber board chair in 1924 and owner of Polar Ice and Fuel, was even blunter: "There's nothing surer than the continued growth and increasing prosperity of Indianapolis."

Local spokesmen were quick to document the case that their confidence rested upon a solid foundation. Writing in *The Indianapolis Star* in March 1921, and using statistics prepared by the Chamber's research bureau, E. V. Parrish presented a series of fifteen profiles that proclaimed the city's "enviable record." Business was booming, up from $1 billion in 1912 to $5 billion in 1920 when judged by bank clearinghouse transactions. Retail sales at the city's 2,300 stores placed Indianapolis thirteenth nationally, while 250 wholesale businesses and over 500 manufacturing firms assured "diversity, stability, and distinctiveness" in the local economy.

Henry L. Dithmer was an active member of the Chamber's board in the early 1920s and board chair in 1924.

Indiana's "Big Four" of the literary world during the early 1900s, as shown in *The Indianapolis Star.* Left to right standing: James Whitcomb Riley and Meredith Nicholson; seated: George Ade and Booth Tarkington.

53

The Grand Old Army Parade, fall
1920, was hosted by the Chamber's
affiliate, the Junior Citizens,
predecessor to the Jaycees.

Yet along with such strong expressions of confidence went voices of caution. Local business leaders were aware of the cyclical nature of the American economy and of the hard times that could result for all if the economy turned sour. The sharp postwar recession of 1919-21 was a strong reminder, particularly in the winter of 1919 when a coal shortage hit the Midwest.

Leaders were also aware that, even with diversity, there were areas of comparative weakness in their own economy. In his profile articles, Parrish felt it necessary to reassure residents about both the comparatively small assets of local banks and the comparatively large dependence upon agricultural processing in the local economic mix. Local leaders often spoke about the need for widespread public support to maintain a favorable climate of opinion in the city. An unnamed advertiser, writing as "a business man who is a resident of Indianapolis by choice rather than by accident," gave blunt, even belligerent, advice in his paid ad in the Chamber's 1926 annual: "If Indianapolis doesn't suit you . . . remember it's one of the easiest towns in the country to get away from. . . . Let's get together—and work together—for Indianapolis first, last, and always."

Membership Initiatives

The Chamber of Commerce reflected this mixture of pride, confidence, and concern in its own activities as the decade opened. In 1919 it launched another major drive to attract new members and to obtain its first multiple-year membership contracts. Numbers rose 10 percent over the wartime highs, and three-year memberships guaranteed a solid dues base until 1922. Yet abruptly in 1922 the Chamber found itself faced with threatened resignations. Eli Lilly and Company, which accounted for over 100 individual Chamber memberships, noted, for example, that it was "not sold on the Chamber of Commerce."

Col. John Reynolds, who became the Chamber's general secretary in 1920, captured the sense of the objections when he noted in the 1920 *Annual Report* that, like the new League of Nations, the Chamber suffered from "the prejudice of the people who think it can do nothing and the support of the people who think it can do everything."

The roots of the problem were undoubtedly those of providing meaningful involvement for the abruptly increased membership. Informal social contacts at the Chamber's rooms and active work by an elected board were clearly insufficient. A proliferation of committees seemed to result in a loss of the clear direction and sense of purpose the Chamber had shown in its formative years. New approaches were clearly necessary.

One was active promotion of a new affiliate, the Junior Chamber of Commerce. Originally called the Junior Citizens (Jaycees did not become a common label until the 1930s), the group proudly traced its origins to World War I and the sense of participation in civic affairs that young men had developed in responding to preparedness and military service. First

Humorist Kin Hubbard was a contributor to the Chamber's monthly report, *Activities*, in the 1920s:

I suppose one of the means, and perhaps the only practical means by which our Chamber of Commerce hopes to build up our city's population and add to its industrial importance, is by proclaiming far and wide its many, many business, cultural and industrial advantages, its fine central location, its parks, good water, shade, steam roads, interurban and bus facilities, factory sites, alluring residence subdivisions, clubs, theaters, schools, barbecues, and general hospitality.

[But] sometimes a little thing is the means of hurting a city or giving it a good name. I don't believe that any tourist who ever ordered coffee along the National Road between Richmond and Terre Haute will ever return to live here. Good coffee leading into a city is just as essential as good paved roads. If any tourists are detouring around Indianapolis, it's on account of the coffee they drink at Greenfield or Plainfield, and not on account of the Wright bone dry law.

The *Heart O' Trade* journal, first published in 1917, moved the Chamber into modern age promotion.

proposed in St. Louis, and officially organized in a national convention in 1920, the group considered itself a bureau of the parent Chamber. The Chamber saw the new association as an excellent training ground for future leaders.

Within Indianapolis, the Junior Citizens showed a clear continuity with the earlier Commercial Club. The first major Junior Chamber activity was to promote a national reunion of the Grand Army of the Republic, locating over 2,000 rooms in the fall of 1920 to house delegates and guests. The second step was to launch a campaign for civic beautification, stressing the need for clean streets and parks.

The Junior Citizens took a role in promoting the Memorial Mall that was emerging along Meridian Street, exposing fraudulent signatures on remonstrances filed against the project. The Junior Citizens were very active in convention and tourism promotion. They attracted and hosted the 1922 national meeting of the Junior Chamber and developed a series of membership meetings designed to acquaint themselves with topics such as business law and commercial banking in a setting that one wit, writing for their newsletter, promised would be "more attractive than the pool room." On the lighter side, they sponsored a number of dances and parties, including a 1923 Halloween Mardi Gras Ball that attracted over 3,000 revelers and a special visit by Rin-Tin-Tin during a motion picture promotion tour to the Circle City. Membership was soon in the hundreds.

The passage of a U. S. Constitutional amendment guaranteeing women's suffrage was a clear indication of the changing role of women in America. The 1920s saw the admission of women to Chamber membership. They quickly became a significant presence in the committee, staff, and leadership structure. Elsie Green had been named assistant general secretary of the staff in 1919 and remained a commanding presence in the office for many years. Natalie Coffin, whose father had been Chamber board chair from 1919 to 1921 (or president, as they were called in those days), became the first woman delegate to the International Chamber of Commerce in 1921. Club women as well as business women were welcomed, and by 1922 more than a hundred were Chamber members.

Staff Development

A second organizational response by the senior Chamber was the professionalization of its staff. Following a national trend toward making chamber offices a reflection of the scientifically managed businesses that they served, new paid staff were hired to perform duties previously undertaken by volunteer committees. A membership secretary, a statistician, and a civic affairs director all joined the staff. The first civic affairs officer, a product of the New York Bureau of Municipal Research, was hired as "an expert in budget analysis and preparation."

Existing members of the staff were soon attending workshops and conferences sponsored by the national Chamber, including a new school for

Nicholas H. Noyes, board chair in 1926, later recalled his years of service: "Our special efforts in those days were watching over current local and state taxes. There were not as many efforts then, as now, to increase them and change them but still constant watchfulness was needed."

Elsie Green, assistant general secretary of the Chamber from 1920 to 1926 and the first woman to hold such an office, is shown in the city's Centennial Parade on June 7, 1920.

Top: A horse and carriage stand ready for passengers at Wood Livery in Indianapolis.

Bottom: Hoosier Motor Club auto show on Monument Circle, June 1908.

Chamber of Commerce secretaries attended by Colonel Reynolds in 1921 and 1923. Improved record keeping and better followup on correspondence became priorities. One unnamed staff member did need to be granted a leave of absence to recover from overwork.

Improved communication was another response of the Chamber to its membership situation. Convinced that many members were simply unaware of the variety and effectiveness of the Chamber's work, the group tried to strike a balance between its historic commitment to quiet promotional activity and its need for membership awareness.

Chamber publications were improved. Newspaper inserts and annual reports were joined by an important new venture. A monthly magazine, *Indianapolis Chamber of Commerce Activities* (incorporating the earlier journal *Heart O' Trade*),was sent to all members. Printed on glossy stock, illustrated by photographs and cartoons, and supported by a number of local advertisers, *Activities* documented both the "brilliant record of achievement" of the Chamber (the title of their 1925 *Annual Report*) and the benefits of the parent city. A regular city business directory, designed to alert members to one another's products and services and to encourage "home buying," soon followed. Display space was set aside in the Chamber rooms for local wares.

Social activities received special attention as the Chamber continued to enhance its membership benefits. The annual dinner emerged as a major event on the city's social calendar, and the cafe at the Chamber's headquarters was enthusiastically promoted as a luncheon center. A new manager brought both a new decor and a health-oriented menu that featured natural foods, a calorie count for every dish, and weekly tips on weight reduction and sensible diet. "Eating for Efficiency" became the cafe slogan. By 1924 the Chamber proudly noted that half of all noon luncheon meetings in the city were held in the cafe.

The improvements were successful. Membership rebounded from its brief 1922 drop, reaching a high of 6,000 individuals in the fall of 1926 after an "Indianapolis First" campaign had added 2,500 new members. The Chamber was among the top ten nationally in members and first in members per capita for the rest of the decade. The organization made the switch from individual to corporate memberships in the 1930s.

The Automobile Era

Simultaneous with its internal reorganization, the Chamber involved itself with a number of projects designed to confirm the leadership that it sought for Indianapolis. High on its agenda was the automobile.

The auto had come to Indianapolis, as it came to several Midwestern cities, as a natural transition from two earlier industrial activities: the manufacture of carriages and of machinery. At first, the marriage of the two involved little more than mounting a gasoline engine, common in the

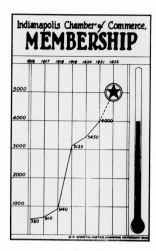

The keynote of the 1920s was business and industrial expansion. This chart, printed in the Indianapolis Chamber of Commerce *Activities* in the early 1920s, showed the decade's rising prosperity for both the city and the Chamber.

Gasoline engine vehicle built by buggy manufacturer Charles H. Black (whose middle initial was incorrectly recorded on the float) in 1891. Is this the missing link in the "marriage of the buggy and the machine?"

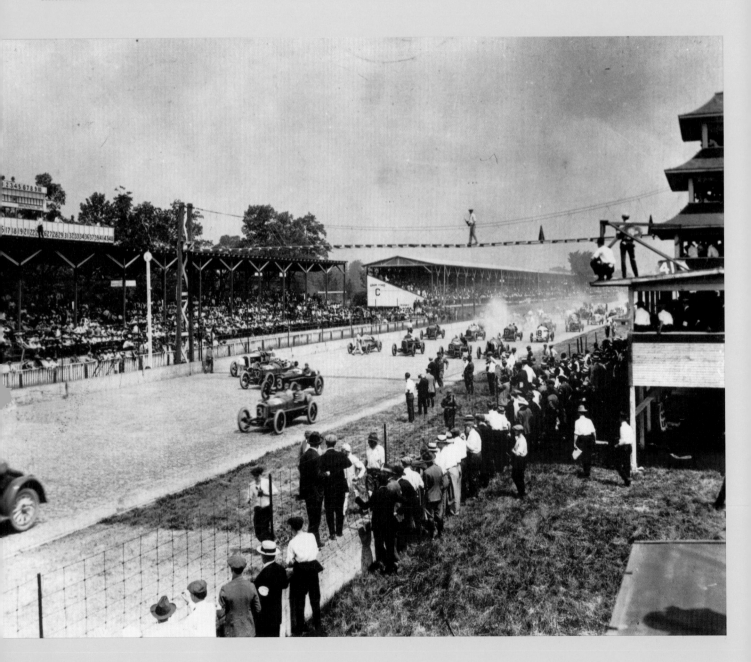

American farm and shop, on a carriage body—a simple activity that could be performed in a backyard shop.

Quickly, however, the automobile became a business in its own right, attractive to growing numbers of Americans. Its declining cost made it accessible to ever wider segments of the public. It was relatively easy to build and market; one could order parts from separate suppliers on credit and assemble a finished car quickly in a small garage for a cash sale through a local retailer. It was especially attractive to mechanically minded Midwesterners, who enjoyed experimenting with everything from styling to performance.

Indianapolis bid aggressively for the new automotive industry. Detroit was to become the assembly center in the 1920s, but the Indiana capital was a major center of everything from the manufacture of parts to the production of prestige vehicles. Famed makes such as the Stutz and the Duesenberg, important publicity events such as the Indianapolis 500, and significant inventions, improvements, and promotions by such men as James Allison, Carl Fisher, and Howard Marmon all attested to the automobile's local appeal and success.

The Chamber's Automobile Initiatives

It was natural for the Chamber to promote the industry. Auto shows under Chamber sponsorship had begun in 1910. By 1920 the Chamber noted that automobile production was already a mainstay of the city economy, with 96,500 being produced by ten local firms. Calling Indianapolis the "Quality Car City Of America" at trade shows and auto fairs, the Chamber proudly noted the city was second only to Detroit. Further, the market for cars, both domestic and foreign, was still growing. *Activities* noted, "The only place we have noted where the saturation point has been reached in the automobile situation is not in the market, but on Meridian Street in the evenings."

The Chamber's 1923 auto show was described in *Activities* as "a fairyland of color and light." The "bunkless and junkless" 1924 show epitomized the eager promotional activity of the era. Both shows promoted retail sales and parts manufacturing as well as assembly.

Hand in hand with marketing went support for use of the automobile. A Chamber committee in 1923 rejected the idea of a city festival to precede the 500-Mile Race, but the race itself was regularly promoted and endorsed in Chamber activities. When local hotels attempted to raise rates for the 1917 race, the Chamber intervened before track owner Carl Fisher could carry out his threat to move the event to Cincinnati. In 1920 the Chamber organized the Citizens' Speedway Committee and initiated the practice of raising funds to pay lap money prizes. The group raised $20,000 in the first year. The Chamber similarly took the lead in 1923 in opposing a law proposed by rural representatives that would have banned racing on Memorial Day. At a time when cars made in

The 1925 edition of *Activities* illustrates the Chamber's promotion of the city as the "Quality Car City of America."

The two most notable "prestige" vehicles, the Stutz and the Duesenberg, were produced in Indianapolis.

Ray Harroun won the first 500-Mile Race in 1911 driving the Marmon "Wasp" made in Indianapolis.

The 1921 Industrial Fair had 400 exhibits and over 100,000 visitors. The successful fair is a testament of the Chamber's original and lasting support of the Indianapolis business community.

Indianapolis were among winners at the race, it was a natural community of interest.

The Chamber argued for a community of interest with rural Indiana as well. It campaigned actively for better roads throughout the state. It welcomed the slogan "Crossroads of America," which originally referred to the crossing of the Lincoln and Dixie highways. The Chamber worked closely with the Hoosier Motor Club to encourage the construction and use of paved roads for both automobile tourism and truck transportation.

Noting that the truck could often go where the railroad did not, the Chamber foresaw major wholesale opportunities for Indianapolis—both as a supplier to outstate Indiana and as a market for agricultural products. With Indianapolis already the largest hog and truck market in America, the Chamber welcomed the arrival in 1920 of the national headquarters of the Motor Truck Owners of North America Association. This, *Activities* noted, would "make Indiana the experimental laboratory for the higher development of motor transport."

In a similar vein, the Chamber encouraged the rise of intercity bus lines, and in a daylong celebration in 1925 helped to dedicate the world's largest bus terminal at West Maryland between Capitol and Senate. With many electric interurban lines beginning to show financial stress, the Chamber was positioning the city for economic change and also confirming its traditional concern for alternatives to waterborne transportation.

Industrial and Community Promotion

Important as automobiles were, the Chamber sought a wider economic base for the city. The group encouraged many forms of business and industry to locate here. They built upon their first industrial survey of 1920 by hosting a major industrial fair in 1921. Displaying many of the 780 articles manufactured in the city, ranging from acetylene gas to xylophones, the fair was proclaimed in *Activities* as "the biggest achievement since the starting of track elevation." Merchants, manufacturers, and citizens were invited to come together under the slogan of "There's Less Wobble At The Hub." The fair attracted 400 exhibitors and over 100,000 visitors during its six-day run in October. In addition to fostering greater product awareness and visibility for a city "in many ways already a world leader," the fair carefully coincided with the national meeting of the National Association of Purchasing Agents. Other fairs followed on a regular basis.

Civic boosterism went in tandem with industrial promotion. Always quick to note Indianapolis as a city of homes, schools, clubs, and churches, the Chamber's publications and programs were rich with evidence of civic achievement. Sports promotion became increasingly com-

The Chamber proclaimed "Indianapolis First" in a week-long campaign to increase its membership and to promote commerce in the city in 1926.

Always ones to love a good show, the members of the Chamber's Indianapolis Day Committee outdid themselves in September 1922 with a special Indianapolis Side Show. The show was set in a labyrinth lined with maps, charts, and information. It opened with a special "Spirit of Indianapolis" pageant. The extravaganza began with a dance by the "imps of pessimism." Then the "City Spirit" routed the imps as it called to the city's aid images of wheat, corn, and coal, "workmen of the city", and "law-abiding citizens." A fireworks finale showcased the Chamber's new motto, "There's Less Wobble at the Hub."

Top: The Chamber of Commerce Building, 320 North Meridian Street, designed in Gothic Revival style, was erected in 1926.

Bottom: Col. John Reynolds, general secretary of the Chamber from 1920 to 1926, shown here in the main office of the new Chamber building.

mon; the city welcomed events ranging from national balloon races to the first national Clay Courts tennis competition.

The most important local campaign was the "Indianapolis First" celebration in 1926. Launched to sell the city and stimulate industry and commerce, it culminated in a weeklong celebration coordinated by the Chamber, which *Activities* proclaimed was the "one local organization with no axe to grind." The campaign was kicked off with a mass meeting at Cadle Tabernacle, featuring self-styled civic evangelist Dan Weigle's "Soul of the City" address. Daily events included civic luncheons, radio broadcasts, and a city-wide Chamber membership campaign that sent its volunteers off each morning to the sounds of marching bands.

A New Building on a Dramatic Mall

Most important, the celebration featured the dedication of the new Chamber building on North Meridian Street. The Chamber had long outgrown its earlier quarters, whose stately elevator speeds were long a subject of local humor. Several locations were proposed for the new building, but the obvious preference was for a site adjacent to the new Memorial Mall emerging between Meridian and Pennsylvania streets north of the old Federal Building.

The mall was an exuberant expression of urban confidence, designed in the form of a memorial to the veterans of World War I. It occupied five city blocks extending north from University Park and contained a number of impressive public buildings centered about a massive World War Memorial. City and state funds were pledged for site acquisition, and both public and private agencies were encouraged to locate their own buildings nearby. In its finished form it is one of the finest examples of "City Beautiful" architecture and planning in America, and it was a natural site for the Chamber's offices.

The Indianapolis Chamber made its most visible contribution by creating a building corporation to erect a new tower at 320 North Meridian Street, where the Chamber would be the principal tenant. The eleven-story skyscraper was designed by Robert Frost Daggett. He used the Gothic Revival style to lend strong vertical lines to the building, which permitted the introduction of elegant structural sculptures and of a spacious "daylight lobby." Many compared the design to the Chamber itself. The design evoked local traditions, because several significant nearby buildings such as Christ Church Cathedral and Second Presbyterian Church were already in the Gothic style. The new building also evoked the Chamber's own spirit of confidence and progress through its clear silhouette and its graceful, ascendant lines.

Civic Challenges and Initiatives

As always, some civic problems demanded solutions even as other civic achievements were celebrated. The Chamber had entered the decade

The Narrative of the City that Started a Booster Campaign

And it came to pass that the merchants and manufacturers of a certain "no mean city" saw a great light in the heavens and a voice spake to them saying: "Go thou and start a booster campaign—that all may see and know the wonders of doing business in the home market."

And lo! in due time a mighty concourse was held. Great was the beating of drums and cymbals and much red fire was burnt. Aye, even unto the seventh day didst the festivities continue with a great increase of revenue to all participants.

But when the shouting was all over, then didst a certain merchant return to his establishment saying: "Now we may rest from our labors and await the coming of multitudes to buy our wares. Thus we may go forth again to distant cities to replenish our stock."

But, behold, in a short time it became evident that even as this certain merchant figured things out—so didst his brother merchants and manufacturers, and great was the howl that went up. For the coveted shekels were going out to strangers, and meantime local merchants and manufacturers were waiting at home for trade that made itself exceedingly scarce.

And when these facts became known then didst this certain merchant and many others rise up in their wrath, saying: "Behold, a one week booster campaign is the bunk. It is a snare and a delusion. I will continue to boost Indianapolis every day in the year and buy from my fellow merchants that they in turn may have the wherewithal to buy from me." And even so, it came to pass.

Robert W. Fleischer
President, Century Paper Company

An engineers' class at Arsenal
Technical High School, circa 1916.
Education on all levels, especially
vocational, was bolstered by the
Chamber in the 1920s when studies showed that the city's labor
force was largely unskilled.

devoting much of its attention to the coal shortage produced by the 1919 miner's strike. The Chamber was the focus for weathering the crisis. It urged stores to close for half days, asked citizens to agree to a skip/stop system of streetcar use, condemned businesses that used coal for non-essentials, distributed conservation posters with the aid of newsboys from *The Indianapolis News,* and lobbied for special help from the Fuel Administration in Washington.

Once coal returned to the city, the Chamber returned to its regular campaigns for a cleaner city. It sponsored everything from a soot-guessing contest ("Who can guess the amount of soot that falls every twenty seconds in the winter on the Mile Square?") to a renewed fire-prevention campaign. Track elevation finally succeeded, with the last grade crossing in the Mile Square eliminated in 1922. Yet new issues soon emerged to replace the old.

One was education. Statistical surveys of the community suggested that about half of the 70,000-member local labor force was unskilled. This disturbing figure pointed to the need for vocational education as a basis for a labor force capable of staffing the new light industries that the Chamber hoped to attract. Vocational counseling in the schools, support for the new compulsory attendance law, and outreach to workers in stores and industries all received Chamber support. Physical plant improvements in the schools and a Scholarship Aid Clearinghouse Committee for needy students followed naturally. Edgar Fowler, director of education services of the U.S. Chamber of Commerce, praised them in the minutes of the local Chamber's Education Committee as aids "to train youth to the complex needs of modern industry."

The Chamber Opposes the Klan

The troubled question of race relations assumed new prominence in Chamber thinking. Indianapolis was a focal point for the Ku Klux Klan activity that troubled many northern and western cities in the 1920s. The state Klan was led by D. C. Stephenson, who attracted members by voicing concerns and fears about new immigrants and new ideas in the city.

The Klan soon entered local politics, where it was successful in several election contests in the mid-1920s. The candidates the Klan supported attempted to implement a social agenda that included segregation in both education and housing. One Klan-backed proposal before the City Council sought to create racial zones of housing in the city which would mirror the racial school boundaries then being established by the school board.

The Chamber and the Klan were often at odds on these issues. Long a champion of reasonable property taxation, the Chamber had no use for school construction that seemed to serve little purpose except that of segregation. Also a champion of home ownership and of adequate housing

Students learn the printing technology of the period in the press room of Arsenal Technical High School, circa 1914, just two years after the school opened as the city's third public high school on the grounds of the old Winona Technical Institute. Winona made the only bid for the Arsenal when it was auctioned by the U.S. Army following the Spanish-American War.

"All for one and one for all" is the slogan adopted for Prosperity day, epitomizing the forward-looking spirit that is coming so much in evidence in Indianapolis.

Proud of the widespread business recovery of the early 1920s, the Chamber celebrated Indianapolis Prosperity Day in August 1922. Mayor Lew Shank declared the afternoon a legal holiday, stores and factories closed, and local residents were treated to aeroplane rides, races, athletic contests, and, yes, speeches. The Chamber took special pride in the holiday as an affirmation of the city's "go-ahead" spirit.

Top: A laborer pot casting ball bearings for an aircraft engine at the Allison Division in the 1930s.

Bottom: The drapery room on the eleventh floor at L.S. Ayres, circa 1928. Lyman S. Ayres, a resident buyer in New York, bought the Trade Palace in 1874 to sell American and European goods. Shortly after the turn of the century, he opened his first store on West Washington Street, replacing the 1845 Hubbard Block building. The L.S. Ayres building at One West Washington was built in 1905.

for the working class, the Chamber saw no good in the idea of racial zones. The Chamber's own task force on housing was firm:

> There can be no question as to the legal right of Negroes to purchase any property on quite the same basis of white people. To refrain from doing so, out of consideration for the preferences of the white race, often seems to Negroes an abrogation of legal status. . . . We strongly recommend that all agitation in reference to this situation on the part of both white and colored groups be discontinued, as we realize the great danger with which such agitation is charged. . . . We . . . request all citizens . . . to assist in creating a cooperative program in reference to Negro housing problems which will assure the continued prosperity of our city.

Apart from the fact that the zoning ordinance was almost certainly an unconstitutional infringement upon property rights, the Chamber argued that such zones would do nothing to improve the housing stock of local workers. The Chamber promptly created a local interracial committee in cooperation with the church federation, publicized their objections through a local housing survey, and offered a series of alternatives that stressed the need to avoid racial confrontation.

The ordinance eventually became a dead letter when a series of investigations of Stephenson, and of local politicians tied to the Klan, resulted in adverse publicity and in indictments and convictions of several leading figures in city government. By the late 1920s the Chamber was taking the lead in proposing alternate candidates who could be relied upon to promote civic cooperation.

The Chamber's response to the Klan typified its approach to the 1920s: a clear recognition of the problems of the period combined with a confidence in the ability of the city to surmount those problems in a spirit of cooperation. Here, as in so many other events in Indianapolis, the 1920s emerged as a decade of change, one in which the Chamber positioned itself for future growth while still acknowledging the fragile structure of the community. It was an approach that would be severely tested in the next decade.

Paul Q. Richey, 1929-30

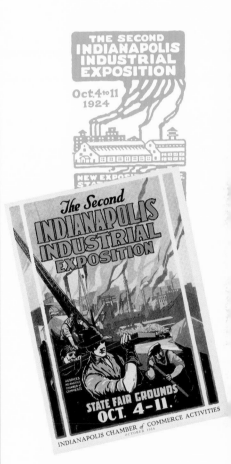

Industrial Expositions staged by the Chamber during the 1920s and 1930s drew hundreds of companies as displayers and attracted thousands of patrons to view the state of local industry.

The Apollo Theatre, September 14,
1940, was located on the east side
of North Illinois Street.

Chapter 4

Depression & War

Economic depression, wartime recovery, and postwar planning became the main themes of Chamber activity between 1930 and 1945. The city was struck by the most serious economic problems in its history, forcing Indianapolis leaders to struggle for well over a decade to preserve the fabric of enterprise and of community in the face of unprecedented economic challenges.

Responses to the Great Depression

Heralded by the stock market crash in the fall of 1929, the ensuing Depression was clearly felt by the summer of 1930. Automotive and other consumer industries were particularly hard hit, as evidenced by the closing of the Stutz and Duesenberg plants. Many other businesses felt the pressures of the time. By 1932 the unemployment rate in the city had risen to over 20 percent, and industrial production had dropped from $427 million in 1929 to $168 million in 1933. Chamber membership itself, often a barometer of business conditions, plunged by three-fourths between 1930 and 1934.

Some commentators in the era treated these conditions as dire harbingers of the future. The leaders of the Chamber did not. Familiar with the cyclical nature of the American economy, and publicly confident in the basic soundness of conditions in Indianapolis, they set in motion a series of relief and recovery efforts that were consistent with earlier Chamber programs.

Part of this momentum flowed from the continuity of membership and leadership that the Chamber enjoyed. In 1940, when it gathered to commemorate the fiftieth anniversary of the Commercial Club, the group was able to honor fourteen living charter members who had remained active over that half century. Chamber committees routinely included members who had gained experience by participating in earlier Chamber projects, and who were prepared to adapt past successes to present problems.

Relief Activity

The Chamber's Emergency Work Committee of 1930 was thus patterned closely after the Chamber Relief Committee of 1893. Like its predecessor, the new committee focused its efforts upon winter months when seasonal unemployment was at its worst. Once again a dole was rejected in favor of a system of public works. Chamber committees repeat-

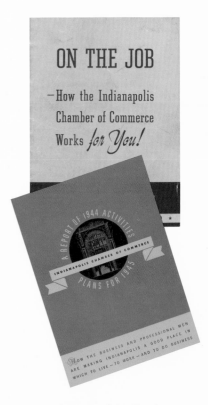

Annual Reports of the Chamber during the 1940s characterized the promotional style of the time.

National Guardsmen board a train in Terre Haute in 1941, preparing for their World War II departure.

71

The Naval Armory, located on
West 30th Street at White River,
was a WPA project completed in
1938.

edly emphasized that aid recipients were treated with dignity and that the community benefited from their work. The Emergency Work Committee minutes noted that the Chamber "keenly appreciates the feelings of some of those citizens of our city who for the first time in their lives will be seeking relief. . . . The whole community has a grave responsibility seeing to it that the adjustment is made with the least possible embarrassment to them."

The new committee copied the previous practice of providing a clearinghouse for jobs offered by private employers and by local government agencies. Those unable to work were referred to other relief agencies whose budgets were subsidized by contributions solicited by the Chamber. Private employers offered jobs that mirrored the employment patterns of the city. Aggregate statistics in 1931 showed 38 percent of the private jobs in building and construction, 22 percent in metals and machinery, 16 percent in transportation, and the remainder scattered everywhere from 3 percent in woodworking to 1.3 pecent in agriculture.

Three public agencies—the county highway department, the city park commission, and the city sanitary district —provided public employment. Together they accounted for about four-fifths of those aided. Originally dubbed "make work" in 1930, the name was soon changed to "emergency work" to more accurately reflect the motives of the program which committee minutes observed "converted public relief into public works."

The range of projects was great. Bricks were removed from older streets to permit asphalt paving, rocks were removed from dirt runways at local airports, Christmas gift toys were repaired for the Campfire Girls, shoes of Wayne Township students were resoled while the children studied, a new channel (dubbed the Panama Canal) was dug for Pleasant Run, and the slopes of Riverside Park were adorned with a rock garden that the minute book said "transformed and expanded it into a hillside of veritable beauty."

Each winter the Emergency Work Committee helped about 5,000 workers, most of whom were unskilled and about half of whom were minority. Each spring the committee evaluated its efforts. It took some pride in providing financial aid, while noting that its efforts did little for the education, clothing, and physical fitness of the workers. The most serious challenge the committee felt it faced was that of worker morale. As a result, it also conducted a varied social program for relief recipients that featured theater showings, football games, and dances.

As in the 1890s, however, the central emphasis was upon feeding the needy. The committee often offered payment in food rather than cash, and sponsored hot noon lunches of coffee, soup, and bread. A special gardening program in 1932 emphasized home food production and used seventy acres of land lent by Butler University as a model site. By the time

Louis J. Borinstein, board chair from 1931 to 1935, later remembered the Depression:

The chief aim of the Chamber during [those years] was to keep it alive. That aim was achieved.

During these years the Chamber played a major part in bringing marked advancement in the relation of Indianapolis with all the forces in the State. This resulted to the everlasting good of Indianapolis and changed the attitude of the rest of the State toward it. There had been a feeling everywhere that Indianapolis wanted to dominate. This was not true . . .

George A. Kuhn, board chair from 1942 to 1943, recalled the war effort: "These were the days of Bond rallies and 'E' awards. There was a mighty effort of all our citizens concentrated on the War Effort—gas rationing—fuel rationing—doubling up in houses—or, shutting off the upstairs to conserve fuel, studying maps and listening to broadcasts to get the latest news on the progress of the War."

Edwin S. Pearce, board chair from 1944 to 1945, added: "Indianapolis made great strides in aviation . . . and the Chamber helped to accomplish this, through cooperation and support from [its] Aviation Committee. With new cross-country air service available when the war ended, Indianapolis quickly became a stopping place on the route of the major airlines going almost any direction, because Indianapolis was located in such a strategic position."

Top: Tomlinson Hall served as a shelter for the homeless during the winter of 1932-1933. An arch on Market Street in front of the City Market is the only visible sign of the grand old building today.

Below: The English Opera House and Hotel, circa 1925, stood as a Victorian treasure on the northwest quadrant of Monument Circle from 1880 to 1950.

its relief efforts were replaced by federally funded programs in 1933, the committee had won national recognition for its "square deal" approach.

Sustaining the Community

After 1933 the Chamber shifted its emphasis to other community problems. The members returned to their traditional emphasis upon adequate housing for unskilled and semiskilled workers. The first sign of this renewed interest was attention to the problem of blankets and shelter for the homeless living in Tomlinson Hall during the winter of 1932-33. Then, in 1934, the federal government indicated willingness to spend $3 million toward the construction of a community housing unit. Citing the additional benefits of employment in the construction industry, the Chamber endorsed the plan.

From here the Chamber extended its concern to other community activities, with particular attention to cultural groups. Noting that the Depression's impact on the box office was particularly acute, the group made an unusually determined effort to support both musical and dramatic groups. In 1934 a campaign for season ticket sales for the Indianapolis Symphony was credited with saving that body from collapse, and in 1940 a similar publicity campaign under the name of the Citizens' Theatergoers Committee of Indianapolis achieved similar success for the Playgoers Group in the English Theater. The Chamber took some pride in subsequent recognition during a Metropolitan Opera radio broadcast as one of the few cities to make serious "contributions to music appreciation."

Defining the Role of Government

The Chamber's concern for the community was real. But such concern did not mean that the group was supportive of every proposal and initiative put forth in the 1930s. The Chamber found itself faced with a growing number of proposals that sought a dramatically expanded role for the government in general and for the federal government in particular.

While never inherently opposed to government action, as their support for housing construction indicated, the Chamber was clearly troubled that many of these proposals were cast in terms antagonistic to the business community or to the idea of enterprise. Proposals to mandate wages, hours, conditions of employment, fringe benefits, and many related topics poured into legislative committees and occupied an increasing proportion of the time of Chamber staff and committees.

Much of the Chamber's response took the form of quiet and unheralded lobbying efforts. Working with a reorganized Indiana State Chamber of Commerce, the organization began to monitor and track state legislation, to alert members to potential problems in proposed bills, and to alert legislators and other government officials to the local Chamber's own legislative program and its concern for the enterprise system.

C. D. Alexander, 1938-39
W. I. Longsworth, 1940-41

Indianapolis Symphony Orchestra, 1940. Members of the Indianapolis Chamber helped preserve the Symphony by supporting a season ticket sales campaign in 1934.

The 500-Mile Race has often been an occasion for special recognition of Indianapolis. In 1941 it helped the Chamber sucessfully attract Honor City recognition from one of America's best known radio programs, *Major Bowes' Original Amateur Hour.*

The Chamber began lobbying in the state legislature for Indianapolis businesses in the 1930s. By the late 1940s, this "grandstand" was set up for lobbyists.

The cumulative effect of these activities was to project the Indianapolis Chamber into the political process as one of the state's significant lobbying groups. From the 1930s forward it was a primary source of accurate economic statistics and a forceful voice on a wide range of legislation that touched upon the Indianapolis community and its business climate. As its image material of the time stated,

> The Chamber is engaged in an organized and continuing program which includes the following objectives: Moderate taxes, fair legislation, and efficient, economical government . . . Attracting new industries . . . Enlarged domestic and foreign markets . . . Equitable freight rates . . . Harmonious relations between employer and employee . . . Public health, sanitation, and fire protection . . . Encouragement of cultural and recreational activities . . . In short, to make Indianapolis a better place to live, to work, and to do business.

Civic Publicity

To complement its quiet lobbying efforts, a major publicity campaign was designed to educate the media and the public about the benefits of business activity and economic freedom. In 1937, for example, the Chamber hosted the editor of *Nation's Business*, Merle Thorpe, to explain how the Chamber could participate "in a nationwide program to bring about a wider understanding of business and its contribution to the national well-being."

The Chamber also renewed its promotional efforts. Once again it produced newspaper inserts and distributed attractive promotional booklets. The 1938 *Indianapolis Today* stressed the themes of social order, civic consciousness, and education and culture as keys to the city's resurgence in commerce and industry. Descriptions of successful local corporations repeatedly emphasized their rise from humble beginnings to current success and invited other new enterprises to join them in Indianapolis.

Ever conscious of the city's dependence upon transportation, the Chamber placed particular importance upon the development of new or expanded opportunities for travel. It publicized the replacement of the city's trolley cars in the early 1930s, supported the introduction of motor buses on new suburban routes, and welcomed the construction of the new transportation shops along White River on Washington Street.

Acting in cooperation with the Works Progress Administration, the Chamber also entered into a study of police cars. Its task force sought to determine the savings that could result from adopting a single manufacturer's car to replace the variety of Marmons, Fords, and Chevrolets that then made up the Indianapolis Police Department's motor pool.

Stressing the cooperation of urban and rural Indiana, the Chamber produced its first route guide, showing all points in the state served by trucks and all motor freight lines serving each point. The Chamber's Rail-

The Chamber's Junior Chamber of Commerce eventually became the Jaycees.

In 1938, the Chamber published a manual for visitors and incoming businesses that served as a tribute to the city's architectural diversity.

Reviving economic conditions in the late 1930s helped to revive business interest in Latin American trade. So did the presence in Central America of Indianapolis author and journalist Meredith Nicholson, the U.S. ambassador to Nicaragua. Through his intervention, President Samoza of that country visited the city and the Chamber in search of improved trade in 1939.

Top: In 1873, mule-drawn street cars like No. 873 were replaced by electric cars, a dream of Commercial Club founder, Col. Eli Lilly.

Bottom: These trolleys, part of the first shipment of trackless trolleys to Indianapolis in December 1932, are lined up in front of the State House prior to the start of a ''christening'' parade. By 1937 Indianapolis had the largest trackless trolley fleet in the country, many built in this city.

road Freight Rate Division assumed regional leadership in mobilizing Midwestern support for a lengthy proceeding in front of the Interstate Commerce Commission to prevent a reorganization of freight rate structures proposed by several Southeastern states. Concern for traffic law awareness led to everything from an interfleet safety competition for truckers to special publications of traffic laws stressing the need to avoid right turns on red. The Chamber even gave its support for parking meters in the context of controlling excessive traffic in the Mile Square.

Aviation Interests

The Chamber also showed interest in the emerging field of aviation. It appointed an aviation secretary, Herbert O. Fisher, as early as 1927, and worked to popularize the new industry in a variety of ways. Fisher himself aided in the selection of the first airport in Marion County, a small field northwest of the city that was purchased by two barnstormers to house their plane. Subsequent Chamber initiatives included support to bring a military airfield to the city, publicity for airmail as a quick means of communication, and support for the formation of a variety of aviation organizations.

Most important, the Chamber participated in the selection of a site for, and in the dedication of, a Municipal Airport west of the city. Road signs were installed directing motorists there and to each of the three private airports that emerged by the mid-1930s. Large arrows on the tops of buildings also directed aviators to the Municipal Airport, which was subsequently named in honor of Col. Harvey Weir Cook, a prominent World War I flyer and the instructor of the first aviation mechanics course at Arsenal Technical High School. In keeping with its interest in trade promotion, the Chamber was also active in attracting commercial airline routes and air freight services to the city. As Herbert Fisher captured the spirit, "There is no doubt that [the Chamber's] aviation department did help mold public opinion and stimulated extreme interest in those early days as it related to local airport legislation and all aeronautical problems."

Industrial Interests

Industrial promotion retained its primacy in the Chamber's program. Rebounding from a 1933 low, industrial production reached $238 million by 1935 and continued to rise through the decade. *Activities* noted in 1937 that the Chamber was concerned that it faced the "danger of falling behind other progressive cities in our efforts to rehabilitate industries and to drive forward for new industries."

In their efforts to encourage that resurgence, staff and board members held firm to their traditional policy encouraging only businesses with a high probability of success in the local economy. One prospect who contacted the Chamber and asked for a cash bonus to relocate in the city was

The Chamber believed these money-eating machines were necessary as a means of traffic control.

MUNICIPAL AIRPORT OPENED FOR SERVICE

City Officials Welcome First Plane.

1,000 VISIT THE FIELD

Brief ceremonies marking the opening of the municipal airport for regular transcontinental service were held Monday afternoon at the port near Ben Davis.

Herbert O. Fisher, secretary of aeronautics of the Chamber of Commerce, appointed a reception committee composed of members of the board of works, the city council, officials of the Pennsylvania railroad and others to greet the first westbound plane of the Transcontinental and Western Air, Inc., when it landed at the field Monday afternoon.

Equipment of the Indianapolis office of the cross-country air lines was moved from Mars Hill airport to the new municipal field, Sunday. More than 1,000 persons visited the new port in the course of the day.

Louis J. Borinstein, president of the Chamber of Commerce, placed on the plane a large postcard, approximately four feet by five feet, addressed to the mayor of Los Angeles, announcing opening of the new Indianapolis port.

Top: Four Indiana aviation pioneers relax for photographers after the dedication of the Indianapolis Municipal Airport on February 16, 1931. Left to right: Herbert Fisher, secretary of aviation for the Indianapolis Chamber and director of Indiana Air Tours; Howard Maxwell, Indiana National Guard and Central Aeronautic Corporation; Charles E. Cox, Jr., manager of Indianapolis Municipal Airport; and Bob Shank, president and owner of Hoosier Airport.

Bottom: The Administration-Hangar Building at the new Indianapolis Municipal Airport was a streamlined, modern facility in 1931.

peremptorily rejected with a public statement that the Chamber refused to participate in a bidding war, even with sound business ventures.

Brief, factual, informational mailings to a carefully selected prospect list were followed by extensive personal contacts. The Chamber used two main criteria with prospects. One was the financial base of the business, essential in a decade when banks were often unable to provide extensive investment capital. The other was, again quoting *Activities* from 1936, "to avoid contacting industries with antiquated employment methods, the type that would refuse cooperative fair dealings with existing sources of employment."

Several successes followed, starting in 1935 with major expansion of the two General Motors plants in the city. The ensuing publicity engendered more inquiries than in any year since the 1920s and helped attract later businesses such as International Harvester in 1937. An updated industrial directory prepared in 1940 listed more than 700 firms active in the city.

The Bill Book Era

The new vitality of the city was mirrored in a new sense of energy in the Chamber itself, particularly after William "Bill" Book assumed the post of executive secretary in 1934. Book had started his career as a cub reporter for *The Indianapolis News* in the 1920s. In 1926 he had become the business manager of the Indianapolis Public Schools, where he had opposed Klan attempts to secure vendor contracts for their supporters. Impressed by his integrity and efficiency, the Chamber had named Book to head their Civic Affairs Committee, and Gov. Paul McNutt had named him state director of unemployment relief in 1933.

Book brought a reputation for hard work, firm principles, integrity and humor to the position. He was quiet and tactful in his dealings, in the tradition of William Fortune and other Chamber leaders who touched with success the projects they supported.

Book set in motion a major reorganization of the Chamber. He argued that success in its varied programs required departmentalization, better budget controls, and a larger membership base with a dues structure adequate to support programs comparable to chambers of commerce in other major cities. He was a particular advocate of cooperation between business and government in the interest of efficiency and integrity. His twelve-point program of 1934 included such traditional Chamber goals as fair taxation, housing renewal, traffic safety, and scientific research. He also favored cooperation with federal authorities to promote world trade, secure loans for business, and promote slum clearance.

Some of Book's actions were internal responses to the Depression. The Chamber's second floor dining room, for example, which had closed for lack of business in the early 1930s, was converted into new offices for the Traffic Bureau and other groups that were promoting recovery.

"City Greetings Go By Air," February 26, 1931.

Asked late in his career to enumerate the Chamber's primary achievements, William "Bill" Book responded that the best accomplishments were those "things that probably would not have happened otherwise":

- a distinctive slum clearance program
- a modern postwar sanitary system
- adequate flood control legislation
- county-wide metropolitan planning
- the new City-County building
- a major fund drive for a modern hospital
- a community attractive to business through fair taxation
- unparalleled business and industrial growth

The Indianapolis Chamber celebrated its fiftieth anniversary in
grand style in 1940, paying special
tribute to William Fortune.

Seated at the Indianapolis Chamber's fiftieth anniversary banquet
at the Claypool Hotel on the
evening of Friday, January 26,
1940, are (left to right) William
Fortune, Fowler McCormick, C. D.
Alexander, W. I. Longsworth and
C. R. Morrison.

Except for a few high-visibility projects, the Chamber under Book pursued its objectives in a traditionally quiet, low-key manner. George S. Olive, reelected board chairman in 1936, noted, "The primary jobs of the Chamber boil down to keeping the town reasonably taxed, keeping reasonably stable labor relations, and trying to keep good government. On those three points, we can get a lot of help from other people and we don't care whether we get any credit."

One board member, elected in 1938, exclaimed in the minute book, "The Chamber of Commerce has hid its light under a bushel. I had no appreciation of the service the Chamber was rendering to the community. It needs publicity."

A Fifty-Year Record

By 1940 the community was clearly rebounding from the effects of the Great Depression. In the case of the Chamber, its fiftieth anniversary dinner offered an excellent opportunity both to look back upon achievements and to initiate discussion of future projects. Meeting at the Claypool Hotel (on the site of the Bates House where the Commercial Club had been founded), more than 700 members honored the 238 businesses in the city which had been founded before 1890 and recognized the 14 remaining charter members of the Club. Fowler McCormick, second vice-president of International Harvester, asked the keynote question, "Why is Indianapolis Successful?" He answered it by emphasizing the close ties of geography and transportation on the one hand, and the character of local citizenry on the other: "It is the essential Americanism of the city, the tradition of individual leadership in government and the arts, and the outward looking commercial spirit. . . . The Chamber of Commerce is the first manifestation of businessmen joining together and looking beyond their own factory gates, thinking, planning, and working for the common good."

In covering the event, *The Indianapolis News* added that local business had "survived and prospered chiefly because of the Chamber's fine commercial and general welfare leadership . . . the people are glad to acclaim the Chamber as the dominant force in this progress.

Wartime Activity

By 1940, of course, the growing threat of war had again directed attention to the question of military production and procurement. Predictably, the Chamber looked to its own record in World War I and again showed interest in linking local producers with government contractors. The Chamber worked through public officials rather than opening a Washington office. Staff members spent considerable time instructing and aiding local businesses, especially smaller firms, in the complexities of government paper work. By 1941 more than seventy local firms accounted for over $600 million in contracts. Indianapolis again ranked among the top

In honor of her husband, Mrs. William Book unveils a street sign dedicated in his name.

Fowler McCormick, second vice-president in charge of manufacturing at International Harvester, summarized the Chamber in his address at the fiftieth anniversary dinner: "To me, looking backward over 50 years to the foundation of the Chamber of Commerce, it seems that perhaps the most important thing about it—or any other chamber—is that the chambers of commerce of this country were the first manifestation of businessmen joining together and looking beyond their office windows, beyond the gates of their own plants, and thinking, planning and working for the common good."

84

ten American cities in war production. More than half of all city companies produced some items for military use.

Assistance to local firms also included advice on conversion to war production, establishment of training schools for plant guards, and efforts to discourage out-of-town firms from raiding the local labor force. The Chamber also took the lead in urging the recruitment of women workers. Working with local schools, the Chamber sought to provide training that would equip workers with new or enhanced skills needed for the increasingly technical production of war materials.

As the shortage of skilled workers grew with the war, a cooperative plan among manufacturers through the U.S. Employment Service Office provided trained workers from existing firms to be supervisors in new plants opening in the city. Other cooperative efforts with government agencies included war bond sales campaigns, scrap metal drives, office space and staff support for rationing boards and war councils, and conservation and safety programs. The Chamber sponsored the Army War Show, which played to at least 100,000 at the Butler Bowl, and adopted an emergency transportation plan that staggered plant opening hours to ease the pressure on mass transit. Some unusual opening times persisted long after the war at Eli Lilly and other companies as a reminder of that effort.

In keeping with its longtime emphasis on adequate worker housing, the Chamber also stressed new home construction. By 1941, housing starts reached 4,000 units annually. The Chamber's non-discrimination policy enabled it to develop a program to minimize discrimination in hiring workers. It then conducted a series of workshops among plant managers to suggest ways to reduce workplace antagonisms toward minority and women employees.

Planning for Peacetime

Of longest-term significance, the Chamber began as early as 1941 to ask what the postwar city might become. A ten-year capital development campaign was soon begun. It charted capital needs for urban growth and allowed the Chamber to direct the attention of business to the problem of maintaining stability at war's end, when government contracts would dry up. The central conclusion of these early planning studies was that the city would best be served by local control. The postwar planning report observed that "in developing first our defense and then our war economy, we have undertaken to use our own initiative as far as possible and not depend on direction and leadership from Washington. In developing the postwar economy we shall, while working with our public officials in essential activities, depend as far as possible on the private capital and enterprise and leadership of our own community."

Given its enduring concern for housing and urban services, the Chamber study identified suburbia as a major challenge of coming years. Housing construction, especially along the streetcar lines, had long reached

Opposite: Western Electric assembly line, 1950. By 1950 women made up 35.4 percent of the Indianapolis work force as a result of efforts to expand that force during World War II.

Children from School #37 collected scrap metal for money to assist manufacturing efforts during World War II.

Many Indianapolis lives have touched the Chamber of Commerce Building. James Farmer tells this account of the war years:

James E. Farmer
That Reminds Me!

A BARBER'S FRIEND: Just before World War II broke, Barber Alvin L. Blankman bought a barber shop in the Chamber of Commerce Building. But then Blankman was called into military service and it looked like his "dream shop" investment would be lost.

Blankman had no one to run the shop for him until a regular customer, who had offices in the same building, volunteered to handle it for him. The customer kept books and made purchases for the four long years Blankman served in the Army.

When the youthful barber donned his white jacket again he not only knew his investment had been carefully protected, but also that the shop's operation had been handled with top efficiency. The reason was that the befriending customer was Bowman Elder, one of Indiana's leading business men.

Top: The Indianapolis Chamber worked to provide stable jobs for soldiers returning home from World War II.

Bottom: The ''Schools at War'' campaign was one of the many World War II projects encouraged by the community and the Chamber.

and passed the boundaries of Center Township in several areas. But urban services, such as sewers and local schools, had been slow to follow.

Consolidation of city and county government in some form was suggested as a solution, particularly in the area of unified metropolitan planning—for which the joint committee on postwar planning, named by the Chamber and the mayor's office, was a pilot group. Concurrently, the Chamber expressed concern for the continued vitality of the downtown business district, as population sought the suburbs, and for racial harmony, as the minority community grew in size.

Concern for the returning soldier was another major Chamber theme. It was often cast in terms of providing employment while avoiding "makework." In 1943 the Chamber's Committee for Economic Development invited each industrial plant to undertake an internal study of its postwar conversion needs. The press release asserted that "this immediate planning is the keynote to making the postwar economy function through private enterprise."

Weaving together these plans, the Chamber developed a master plan for public improvements that would be needed to serve both business growth and an expanded city.

In 1944, as the war drew to a close and the planning activities were in high gear, the Chamber prepared a color motion picture. *Busting Out at the Seams* captured the spirit of optimism that ran through the development plans. The silent film, which was shown with an accompanying narration by a Chamber speaker, contrasted the orderly treatment of urban affairs in the city of Indianapolis with the disorderly problems of suburban growth, ranging from shacktowns to open dumps. It sought to convince all local residents of the benefits of annexation and county-wide planning.

The Chamber thus entered the postwar era with confidence. It had both a clear philosophy and a specific set of priorities and proposals that looked ahead to planned growth. Its program suggested how well central Indiana had responded to the challenges of depression and war.

C. E. Whitehill, 1946-47

Indianapolis business growth had reached an all-time high by mid-1945, according to a report by Promotion Appraisals, a business research organization in Indianapolis.

The Indianapolis Chamber made
the services of its staff and all its
facilities available to postwar
Indianapolis. This scene at
Meridian and Washington Streets
illustrates Indianapolis' return
to a thriving commercial center
by 1946.

Chapter 5

Postwar Challenges

Hopes were high as Indianapolis tackled the long list of community needs that had emerged during the years of depression and war. Despite their best planning efforts, however, the Chamber and its members found themselves faced with problems whose complexity strained traditional approaches and methods while requiring innovative ideas and tactics.

The postwar Chamber drew upon a strong membership base, now anchored in business firms rather than individual members, to meet these challenges. Participation accurately reflected the diversity of the economic community by 1946, when the membership rolls showed 25 percent in manufacturing, 20 percent in retailing, 15 percent in wholesaling, 11 percent in service, 8 percent in professional activities, another 8 percent in real estate and construction, 5 percent in insurance, and 3 percent in financial services. Overall membership thereafter remained at high levels, with slow but steady growth.

The postwar Chamber's organization reflected its historic interests. The major staff and committee responsibilities focused upon administration, civic affairs, government and public affairs, industrial and business development, and law enforcement and safety.

Enterprise and Education

The first of the unexpected challenges of the postwar years was the appearance, both locally and nationally, of strong attacks upon the American enterprise system. The attacks stemmed from various sources, ranging from individuals angered by the suffering of the Great Depression to advocates of the ideologies of the political left. The critics often differed among themselves upon details, but all professed a lack of confidence in the ability of business to maintain a strong peacetime economy.

Viewed from the perspective of later decades, such critics can be seen as a vocal minority who did not enjoy wide public support. But viewed in the context of the immediate postwar years, when the issues related to the Cold War and Communist Russia attracted daily headlines, the critics became a matter of deep concern to Chamber leaders. It was a measure of the concern that the board was moved to note in 1948 that "the most fundamental necessity today is preserving the free enterprise system against all attacks."

Two years later, board chairman (1951-52) J. Ralph Fenstermaker expressed similar concern in his address, "This We Cherish, This We

Two past chairmen of the board of the Chamber congratulate J. Ralph Fenstermaker after his reelection as board chair in December 1951. Left to right: George S. Olive, J. Ralph Fenstermaker and Howard J. Lacy II.

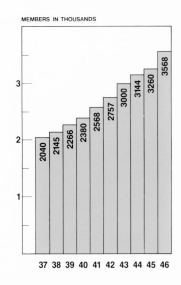

Membership Growth 1937-1946

MEMBERS IN THOUSANDS

Year	Members
37	2040
38	2145
39	2266
40	2380
41	2568
42	2757
43	3000
44	3144
45	3260
46	3568

In the late 1940s, the Indianapolis Chamber gave special attention to secondary education, initiating several ongoing programs. One program sent high school students to local businesses, such as the above field trip to Eli Lilly and Company.

Defend." He identified two challenges, stemming from "those who for selfish reasons seek to destroy free enterprise and personal liberty, and those misguided, ill-informed persons with crusading tendencies and crackpot ideas, who seem to believe that utopia can be reached by confiscating the rewards achieved by men of vision and initiative."

The Chamber was, of course, concerned that antibusiness attitudes would eventually lead to ill-conceived and hostile laws and government regulations. It was even more concerned that hostile attitudes would grow among rank-and-file citizens. Chamber leaders repeatedly expressed confidence in the underlying good sense of the public. But they also expressed alarm at widely held public misunderstandings of the free enterprise system—misunderstandings which the Chamber felt it had a special responsibility to correct.

To counter such perceived challenges, the Chamber launched several initiatives after 1947. Well-publicized lecturers appeared under Chamber sponsorship with increasing frequency. Henry Taylor spoke on "Looking Ahead at Home and Abroad," William Clayton spoke on "The Marshall Plan," and Ralph Bradford lectured on "Last, Best Hope of Earth." Informational pamphlets provided statistics and insights into the workings of the postwar recovery to a varied range of executives, educators, and journalists.

The New America, a "grandiose color picturama" prepared by *Life* magazine, used five projectors and a forty-foot-wide screen to display American resources and productivity to local audiences. A speakers group, the Minutemen, trained over eighty business leaders including "many capable women," who presented short speeches on the enterprise system to local schools, churches, and clubs. Drawn together as The American Opportunity Program, it was a clear indication of the extent of Chamber concern.

Building on this success, the Chamber next inaugurated a Community Education Division to continue such work. In ensuing years, the division expanded the speakers program, distributed numerous films, and began extensive plant visits. Business Education Day continued for over a decade. The event featured visits by teachers to local businesses; it was accompanied by workshops and the subsequent distribution of films. Quick to sense the emerging power of new technology, the Chamber began broadcasting television programming in 1953 with the series *American Town U. S. A.*

On occasion, the Chamber concerns were expressed in negative attitudes. At one point it created a committee to investigate "subversives" in state universities, and at another charged that a widely used government textbook promoted socialism. Most Chamber programs, however, were informational and patriotic in character, stressing the inherent strengths and opportunities of the country and its economic system. The Chamber, in fact, won extensive national publicity for its wide-ranging efforts. One

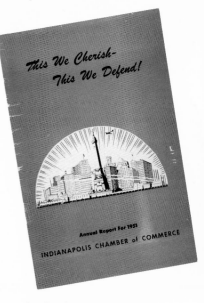

The Chamber's *Annual Report* for 1951 points to the benefits of a free enterprise system in the late 1940s and early 1950s.

Business Education Day won friends for the Indianapolis Chamber in many ways. Here's what two of the teachers later said:

I had always had a definite idea . . . that your [Chamber] office was staffed by cold-hearted business men who sat around nights planning how to keep teachers' salaries from being raised. . . . I found . . . a group of warm-hearted people who were vitally interested in doing everything possible to improve their services to the city and people in it.

I shall always think of the Chamber as comprised of energetic, well-trained folk who are seeking the best for the community and are giving it the best they have!

J. Ralph Fenstermaker at a point along the Communist Iron Curtain that separated Eastern Europe from the free world during the Cold War years. Fenstermaker was one of sixty prominent Americans on a study tour of Radio Free Europe facilities at the time this picture was taken in the fall of 1959.

visiting editor captured their approach when he called them "evangelists with your feet on the ground."

The special concern for enterprise education in Indianapolis soon broadened to a desire for school growth and improvement. A school and industry committee worked to improve science and mathematics education. It raised funds to send teachers to summer institutes and provided them with local summer employment opportunities in scientific corporations. Student field trips to major industries, especially Allison and Lilly, became a major activity and pointed in turn to a renewed interest in vocational education.

Demobilization and Growth

Responses to changed attitudes were accompanied by responses to changes in the economy itself. The Chamber had anticipated problems of postwar demobilization but was surprised by the extent of change. However, not all of the surprises were unhappy. Many who had migrated to the city during the war remained thereafter. They joined returning veterans and the postwar baby boom to spur growth in the city's population. This enlarged labor force—which at 290,000 in 1946 was almost twice as large as it had been before the onset of the Depression—assured ample labor for postwar growth.

Initial concern for maintaining employment levels disappeared, moreover, in the face of postwar prosperity. After the short recession that usually follows a war, Indianapolis rebounded well. The Chamber's 1948 *Annual Report* highlighted the fact that every local business index was at its highest point ever. One national journal had used Indianapolis as a case study of the Midwest city that had achieved the most marked business development.

Several factors contributed to this remarkable growth. One was the ability of local firms to adapt to the new consumer demands of the postwar world. The rapid rise in automobile sales, for example, supported the growth of the city's automobile parts industries. Good labor relations and the relative absence of serious strikes continued to make the city attractive to new or expanded business. The willingness of new types of business, such as the insurance industry, to locate in the city substantially expanded its economic diversity.

Scientific Services

The Chamber was quick to recognize that Indianapolis was in competition with many other cities, including the new cities of the sunbelt that were beginning their own rapid growth in these decades. Much resulting Chamber activity was designed to continue or expand traditional programs that would attract and support viable business activity.

Services to members covered a wide range of individual needs. Assistance was provided to owners seeking new plant locations and to existing

The 1946 Indianapolis Industrial Exposition at Union Station was conceived by Edwin Pearce, the Chamber's board chair from 1944 to 1945. An array of ninety-three glass and aluminum display cases allowed firms to show their products and services to 4,000-10,000 people per day.

◆ TO PRESERVE THE AMERICAN WAY OF LIFE ◆ INDUSTRY MUST EQUIP OUR NATION FOR LEADERSHIP IN A WORLD AT PEACE ◆

HOW ONE CITY SELLS ITSELF

By WILLARD MARSH

ANY traveler by rail who changes trains or stops over in Indianapolis, Ind., and who goes on his way without having learned something about that city is either stone blind or hopelessly intoxicated.

Spurred by a living-and-breathing Chamber of Commerce, Indianapolis civic leaders, business men, labor leaders and industrialists have poured time, elbow grease and money into the establishment of a permanent Industrial Exposition in the train concourse of the Indianapolis Union Station.

This array of 93 beautiful glass and aluminum display cases constantly advertises to the traveling public the products (and the names) of 74 of Indianapolis' more than 900 industries.

A business man or a pleasure traveler passing through Indianapolis can while away minutes or even hours looking at such things as the mysterious inner workings of a transparent plastic telephone set; a color-outlined, cutaway section of an Allison turbo-jet aircraft engine that moves as in actual operation when a button outside the display case is pressed; Surface and aerial photographs of Indianapolis and environs; charts and maps.

Motion pictures with sound to tell the story of Indianapolis to the passing parade will be added soon, it present plans mature. It will be difficult indeed for anyone to visit Indianapolis,

even for a half-hour stopover, without carrying away some knowledge or some impression of that city.

NOW—let's move westward a couple of thousand miles to the verdant shores of beautiful Puget Sound, to lift a handful of words from the advertising brochures.

Seattle and Indianapolis are cities of approximately the same size. The 1940 census named Indianapolis as the No. 20 American city with a population of 386,972 persons. The same census tabbed Seattle as No. 22, with 368,302 persons. Could it be possible that Seattle could learn something of value from a sister American city of similar size?

We have seen how Indianapolis has converted its railway station into a 24-hour-a-day salesman for Indianapolis. Travelers look. They listen. They learn.

They go home remembering Indianapolis as the city where they were entertained and pleasantly instructed while waiting for a train.

Travelers passing through Seattle's railway stations — thousands of them every week — can do just what they do in other railroad stations all over the land from Bellingham to Biloxi and from Pawtucket to San Pedro.

(1) They can wander back and forth to the restroom.
(2) They can memorize the train arrival and departure bulletins.
(3) They can polish benches with their skirts or trousers.
(4) They can try to read.
(5) They can speculate on the probable age of tired-looking apples or oranges stacked up on the lunch counter.

They are bored. They want to get moving. They sigh with relief when their train is announced. They pass through Seattle without knowing anything about this city and they care less. Indianapolis' experience has proved already that a little money and some substantial effort expended in the interest

of municipal promotion — beating, if you will—pays.

It is undoubtedly true that the travelers passing through any American city are just the... But 70,000 a week pass Indianapolis station. And in... there is a certain percentage... ing agents or sales direct... presidents.

SO: Nearly every exhibitor... dianapolis exposition has... valuable sales contacts resulting from business executives view... exhibits.

An Indianapolis manufacturer o... ning plant machinery completed... tracts with two firms in India... result of their representatives gettin... caught between trains in the Indianapo... lis station, during which time they saw scale models of canning-plant equipment manufactured in Indianapolis.

A contractor from Oregon stopped, looked—and ordered earth-moving and paving equipment manufactured in Indianapolis.

The manufacturer of a new, automatic home-laundry machine reports he has obtained new distributors and new sales outlets as a direct result of the display. Backers of the exposition are so pleased with public acceptance that they are planning now to construct additional displays.

THERE are differences that would have to be adjusted should any civic or business group in Seattle decide to sell this city to the traveling public in the same manner.

In the first place, Seattle has two stations. There might be additional expense in establishing two separate "Let's-Have-a-Look-at-Seattle" expositions. But Indianapolis' experience would indicate that even a double display should pay off in extra business, new industries and the good will of passing travelers.

And what about Bow Lake Airport?

Is it possible that Seattle and Tacoma could back a joint "Puget Sound Exposition" where travelers from all over the world one day will pass by?

Indianapolis has shown the way.

TRAVELERS gather about displays in the Indianapolis Union Station exposition, keenly interested in the mechanized, colorful exhibits of the things that are made or processed in Indianapolis plants.

A VIEW of the front ends of six of several island cases, each containing ten separate exhibit spaces. The display cases are constructed in the form of modern, streamlined railroad cars. They are made of aluminum and molded crystal glass.

ENGINEERS: By pushing a button, spectators can operate a cutaway Allison turbo-jet aircraft engine. The engine displays a full and fully explained view of the internal working parts and mechanism.

"You won't get away with this!"

THE SEATTLE TIMES, SUNDAY, AUGUST 24, 1947. 5

94

firms that sought to contain costs. A detailed industrial analysis in 1953 sought to identify gaps in services to area businesses which new firms might fill. The emphasis on scientific study of business conditions was reflected in continued statistical surveys and the expansion of the Chamber library to provide statistical resources to local firms.

The emphasis on careful statistical study earned the Chamber a good reputation for care and accuracy. In 1946, for example, Carl Dortch, a staff member for more than forty years and president from 1964 to 1979, reviewed the city government's budget—already approved as the basis for property taxation in 1947—and discovered that the omission of repayment for an outstanding loan had resulted in an error of $1,070,000, which no public auditor had caught.

Suburban Growth

The Chamber showed a special interest in postwar zoning and land use, particularly as residential growth began to suggest the difficulty of maintaining future industrial tracts within the county. Representatives of the American Society of Planning Officials consulted with Chamber staff to produce a comprehensive revision of city zoning ordinances. A large number of variances had been sought each year, and the result was piecemeal zoning. Now the Chamber endorsed a new ordinance, adopted in the mid-1950s, which made possible large tract zoning under a county-wide authority.

The most visible result of the new zoning was the rise of suburban industrial parks in Marion County. In 1961 Samuel Fletcher planned the first such park on a 625-acre tract near the airport. The Chamber took an active role in this effort. It created a special committee to deal with neighborhood relations, personally notified each of the 200 or more adjacent property owners, and hosted community meetings to explain the planned development. The subsequent dedication of Park Fletcher was a joint triumph for the developer and for the Chamber's approach to development. As Fletcher himself concluded, he "had never found a city where there was such excellent cooperation between public officials and the Chamber of Commerce."

Renewed Trade Promotion

The Chamber's special delight in industrial and trade shows continued. In 1946 it opened the permanent Indianapolis Industrial Exposition at Union Station. The exhibit permitted local firms to display their products, services, and messages in attractive display cases. The show was ostensibly designed for the business traveler. Nonetheless, it drew a large audience which eventually totaled between 4,000 and 10,000 per day.

The Chamber concentrated anew on world trade, particularly with Latin America. Interest had been piqued both by the growth of exports (up to $25 million by 1944) and by the continued Pan-American interest evinced in wartime festivals and celebrations. Beginning in 1946 a num-

J. Ralph Fenstermaker, 1951-52
Howard J. Lacy, II, 1953-54

J. Ralph Fenstermaker, board chair in 1951 and 1952, summarized the group as "determined that it was our obligation to prove, by information and by example, that the traditional economic system offers rewards for those willing to do their job and that local communities working toward the solution of their own problems could perform better without the intervention of a . . . federal bureaucracy."

Fenstermaker also noted the Chamber's continued application of scientific principles to the reception of the Army Finance Center: "The Chamber urged that Indianapolis be considered only if it served the public and national interest and was the proper site under strict economic considerations. No effort was made to use political persuasion; in fact, such was avoided. The military decision-makers rewarded our community in this novel and basically sound approach."

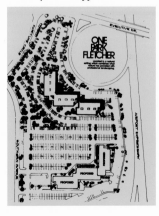

The Chamber believed that large tract zoning, such as One Park Fletcher, would balance residential and commercial land development.

The old Marion County Court-
house stood beside the new, tower-
ing City-County building for
several days before the older
building was demolished in 1962.
The Indianapolis Chamber
encouraged the eventual merger
of city and county governments.

ber of trade tours flew numerous business leaders throughout Central and South America to discuss the export of Indiana agricultural and industrial products. Translation services, aid with travel documents, and information on foreign trade regulations soon became a regular feature of staff activity. Classes in business Spanish soon followed.

Government for City—and County

Closer to home, the Chamber continued to suggest paths for urban governance and development, working from the earlier wartime proposals. The primary focus was upon establishing metropolitan planning which would serve Marion County, as well as the city of Indianapolis.

Such a focus drew the Chamber into extensive work with the Indiana General Assembly, which, in the absence of home rule for cities and counties in Indiana, had original jurisdiction over most of the proposals the Chamber advanced. The legislature had not been redistricted since 1921, and it showed a marked rural flavor in those years. It was indifferent, if not hostile, to Indianapolis interests. Bills often languished in committee, and progress was slow at best.

Nonetheless, several key proposals eventually did become law. Each provided a county-wide authority to deal with a specific area of governmental responsibility. Among these were agencies for development planning, health and hospital services, and airport authority. Most visible was the creation of a separate authority to erect a common city-county building to replace the older City Hall and Court House, a project brought to successful completion in 1961. Carl Dortch, in a letter to the Evansville Chamber of Commerce concerning the partial merger of city and county functions, said, "Through all this experimentation with metropolitan government we have made a great deal of progress, but the package has a curiously hybrid wrapping around it."

In the meantime, the Chamber continued its interest in the existing city government. The Budget Advisory Committee remained active, particularly when questions of economy in government were proposed. The Chamber continued its long-term emphasis upon a merit system for public employees. Various home rule amendments proposed to the General Assembly advocated the city manager form of government, and numerous plans for better training of the city police force were advanced.

The "hybrid" approach to government often replicated itself in urban development. The city of Indianapolis was growing by a series of annexations, principally to the northeast and northwest, which eventually touched six of the eight outer townships of the county and which had the gradual effect of extending some city services to suburban areas.

Interstate Highways and Local Housing

Apart from its emphasis on zoning, the Chamber's most important responses to such changes were in the areas of roads and housing. The Chamber became the leading advocate of interstate highway construction after the adoption of the Interstate Highway Act in the mid-1950s. The

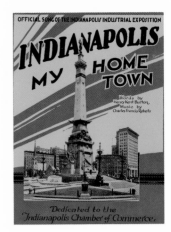

"Indianapolis, My Home Town," by Henry Kent Burton, was dedicated to the Indianapolis Chamber and was the official song of the Indianapolis Industrial Exposition in 1946.

Indianapolis flourished in the postwar period. One of the many permanent innovations of the time was drive-in banks, such as the above Peoples State Bank building that opened in early 1950.

L. E. Kincannon, the Chamber's board chairman from 1969 to 1970, appealed to a county-wide legislative body on behalf of Unigov on January 16, 1969.

Top: Interstate highway construction had the right-of-way in the 1960s. Part of a neighborhood was razed to make way for I-70 and I-65 at Raymond Street during that decade.

Bottom: The Indianapolis Chamber supported the completion of eight major interstates throughout the city. This scene shows the dedication of I-65 and I-70 on Friday, Oct. 15, 1976.

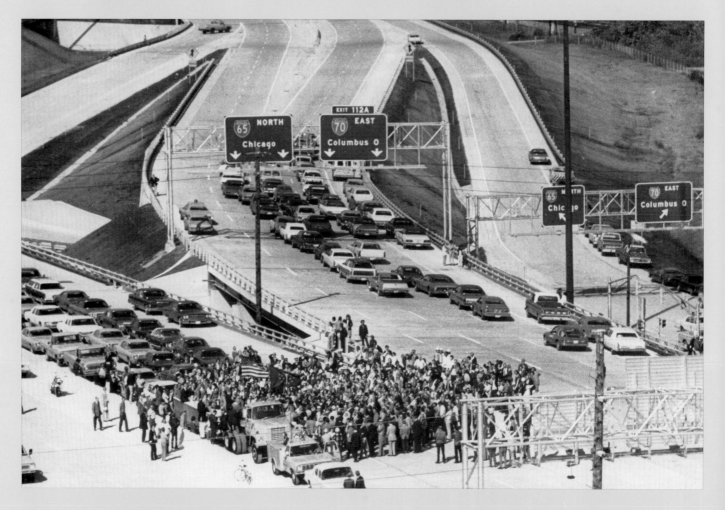

Chamber was eager to quickly finish the seven major interstates—the greatest number reaching any Midwestern city—which converged on Indianapolis. The Chamber was even more interested in planning an interstate system that would reach into the city and serve the Mile Square. The 1957 *Annual Report* foresaw "the imagination-staggering highway and freeway programs whose implementation will shape the pattern of living and doing business in Indianapolis for a hundred years."

Recognizing that a substantial amount of land would have to be removed from commercial and residential use in the city, the Chamber labored long to build public support for the necessary changes. Public forums and extensive negotiation with state agencies followed. The Chamber constantly sought to avoid unnecessary delay from the many changes in proposed routing. As the *Annual Report* asserted in 1957, "The Chamber's role is to cooperate with all and to urge decisions on the difficult issues of location, demolition, and access points."

The Chamber's interest in new roads did not preclude a continued concern for city streets and for the continued issue of railroad track elevation. The Chamber had, of course, been successful in achieving elevation within the Mile Square. Now, after the war, it worked closely with Walter "Doc" Hemphill of the Indianapolis City Council in an attempt to extend this success outward to deal with the Kentucky and Morris Street areas.

Highway work necessarily pointed to housing policy. The projected demolition of several thousand housing units and the need to relocate about 14,000 individuals fed naturally into the Chamber's long-standing interest in urban renewal.

Four key considerations underlay the Chamber's approach to housing. One was a desire to maintain local control of planning, rather than to surrender that control to state or federal authority. The second was to attract sufficient capital to permit the construction or reconstruction of adequate housing stock. The third was to provide sufficient housing to meet the needs of both the returning veteran and the growing population of the city. And the fourth was to avoid the mistakes which the Chamber felt had been made in other cities, particularly in the construction of overly large and unattractive public housing projects.

As early as 1945 the Chamber was successful in obtaining passage in the General Assembly of legislation to create the Indianapolis Redevelopment Commission. Empowered to levy taxes, to acquire and clear blighted areas, and to plan their redevelopment, the Commission members showed skill in developing projects in cooperation with civic groups and associations. In the next twenty years they spent $12.2 million to buy and clear 1,842 parcels of land and to construct 1,221 new housing units and 11 commercial buildings. The Chamber recognized that the interstates would create greater pressure on housing than the Commission could meet; it concentrated on advocating repair and improvement of existing housing stock.

W. Henry Roberts, 1955-56
Joseph O. Waymire, 1959-60

(Previously pictured)
Harry T. Pritchard, 1957-58

Carl R. Dortch played the role of "watchdog" at city hall during his tenure as director of the Chamber's bureau of government research.

The Indianapolis Chamber sought to promote goodwill and trade with Europe in the 1950s. In this scene, members board a TWA flight to Europe in January 1952.

In the 1960s, downtown Indianapolis was just on the verge of an
urban renaissance.

Working with the New York–based Center for Voluntary Action, the Chamber launched a pilot program of inner-city renovation. The New York Life Insurance Company and local investors became involved in the 200-unit project, which stressed the use of minority contractors.

Chamber leaders continued within this context to support the concept of open housing, particularly after a key 1959 meeting that illustrated the group's approach to community action. Asked to comment on an open-housing proposal before the City Council, the Chamber board initially expressed reservations about the legislation. But before taking final action, the board invited a number of leaders of the Indianapolis black community to a special evening at the Lincoln Hotel. There the black community leaders, and particularly the Rev. Andrew Brown, presented a persuasive case for the new ordinance. The Chamber board promptly withdrew its opposition and instead endorsed the measure.

Community Images

The shift to the suburbs helped alert the Chamber to the problems of maintaining business in the Mile Square. A special downtown merchants committee, the Indianapolis Civic Progress Association, was established. It sought to make the downtown area more attractive to shoppers by improving lighting and by cleaning streets that a nationally known writer, John Gunther, had described as "unkempt, unswept, and raw." Concerned that traffic conditions were discouraging shoppers, a special Chamber study indicated a need for new one-way streets and other traffic flow changes.

In a larger sense, community image was central to the Chamber's program in these years. From their vision of an enterprise city to their desire that the interstate highways be a true American crossroads, Chamber leaders were presenting the community in ways they hoped would attract national business. To those ends, much of the staff and committee work of the organization was devoted to the public presentation of the community.

The Chamber's public image of the city achieved clear expression in 1964. It published a special industrial recruitment publication modeled after *Life* and called *Life in Indianapolis*. After its introductory editorial, "An Island of Decency," the magazine looked at the city through the eyes, and words, of six recently arrived families. It was rich in statistics, but stressed the "livable qualities" of Indianapolis. Each personal story spoke of cultural opportunity, educational quality, neighborhood diversity, and economic vitality. The year 1964 also saw the appearance of *News Briefs,* which would later evolve into *Indianapolis Magazine.*

Paul L. McCord, chairman of the Indianapolis Chamber's housing subcommittee, was instrumental in drafting and introducing measures to the General Assembly for slum clearance and urban development beginning in the late 1940s.

A new logo was adopted by the Indianapolis Chamber in the years after the fiftieth anniversary in 1940.

The Chamber's interest in the beauty of the Memorial Mall did not die with its construction between the World Wars. After World War II, Obelisk Square, to the north of the main memorial, became the home of several pieces of war surplus hardware, including a wartime tank and a postwar jet fighter. Initially installed to reflect public patriotism, they decayed over the years to become public eyesores. Concerned, the Chamber staff discreetly contacted the director of the World War Memorial, and the weapons quietly disappeared.

The Sargent Paint Manufacturing Company's float, featuring a Mardi Gras theme with huge jesters and other figures, won the grand prize, the Indianapolis Chamber of Commerce trophy, in the 1964 500 Festival Parade.

VICTORY
AWARD DINNER

★

HONORING THE RACE DRIVERS OF THE 31ST
INTERNATIONAL 500 MILE RACE AT THE
INDIANAPOLIS MOTOR SPEEDWAY, MAY 30, 1947

★

INDIANAPOLIS ATHLETIC CLUB   MAY 31, 1947
7:00 P.M.

UNDER THE AUSPICES OF THE
INDIANAPOLIS CITIZENS SPEEDWAY COMMITTEE
OF THE INDIANAPOLIS CHAMBER OF COMMERCE

Lap prizes for the 500-Mile Race at the Indianapolis Motor Speedway have been sponsored by the Indianapolis Chamber through its Citizens' Speedway Committee since 1937.

New Sports and Arts Promotions

The search to present a positive urban image was also apparent in the changing face of the 500-Mile Race. Suspended during World War II and under new management after the war, the race soon posed the types of challenge that the Chamber was adept at solving. By 1947, for example, the Chamber was taking the lead in promoting better traffic management and parking in the Speedway area. Then, in 1957, the Chamber supported the creation of the modern 500 Festival.

Striving, in the words of the 1957 *Annual Report,* to meet "the long felt need for extra sparkle and glamour," the annual festival included extensive publicity, a variety of dinners and receptions, such special events as a dance on Monument Circle and a parade designed around floats, bands, and local marchers. The Festival was a money maker from its first year and was soon drawing crowds of over a quarter million.

Concern for sports promotion extended to amateur athletics as well. The Chamber regularly held recognition dinners and events. Among these were a special dinner for Butler University coach Tony Hinkle on the occasion of his 500th basketball victory and a series of "Ammy" awards to amateur athletes in ten local sports.

Also interested in professional teams, the Chamber supported ticket sales for the ill-fated United Football League Warriors, and helped induce the Cleveland Indians to sell their Indianapolis AAA baseball team to a group of local investors. By organizing a sale of stock in small units, the Chamber's Athletic Committee involved 6,548 investors and over $200,000 to keep the American Association baseball franchise in the city. Subsequent efforts to expand and improve the local stadium, then called Victory Field, soon followed.

The Chamber also continued its support of local cultural activities. It supported the "Acropolitan" concept which sought, in emulation of the ancient Greek *polis,* to create a cultural center for Indianapolis along the banks of White River on the city's north side. The resulting development included such key institutions as the Indianapolis Museum of Art, the Indianapolis Civic Theatre, Christian Theological Seminary, Starlight Musicals, and Clowes Memorial Hall of Butler University. These cultural facilities were supported through Chamber participation in their ticket sales campaigns and in their opening fund-raising programs.

The Take-Off Years

Viewed in retrospect, the twenty years after World War II displayed a variety of Chamber activities that flowed naturally from its wartime planning. By 1965 these had contributed to what might best be called a "take-off" situation. Indianapolis was now poised to adopt or adapt a number of exciting urban initiatives—and the Chamber was in a position to play a key role in shaping those initiatives.

Wendell Phillippi, longtime managing editor of *The Indianapolis News,* later recalled the role of the Chamber in keeping professional baseball in Indianapolis:

When it was in danger of folding, W. F. (Bill) Fox, Jr. and I went to Bill Book, begging him not to let the Indians fold since it was the only major sports team we had, [with] its long history and the interest of a lot of us in baseball.

Bill, an alumnus of *The News,* listened at first still not convinced. After several sessions and stories, he relented and threw his support to the group. Bob Kirby was chairman of the sports committee . . . and another strong supporter.

As a result we got Frank McKinney (Sr.) to lead the drive and head up the Indiana organization. Public sale of stock saved the team, and *The News* promoted the hell out of it. McKinney did a great thing in his first year in charge: He hired Max Schumacher as ticket manager. Max of course had had a great career in directing our team to four straight championships, and he should get a lot of credit for doing the same.

The Indianapolis Chamber long
supported efforts to expand public
higher education and maintains a
strong relationship with Indiana
University/Purdue University at
Indianapolis (IUPUI).

Chapter 6

A Changing Urban Economy

Indianapolis in the 1960s and 1970s was a city on the move. It countered the national image of Northeastern "rust belt" decay with an urban renaissance that would win national recognition and praise. Acting in partnership with a variety of community groups and individuals, the Chamber of Commerce provided a central pool of interests and talents to lead and support dramatic changes within the city. Ultimately termed an "urban renaissance" by some contemporaries, the changes reflected a broadly based drive to maintain Indianapolis' place among major American cities.

The Chamber's central focus remained the promotion of business and industry and the creation of new job opportunities in central Indiana—a focus that reflected its concern with the turbulent economic conditions of the country after 1965. America's economy was in a growth mode, fueled by the postwar "baby boom" and rapid increases in consumer spending. But the economy was also in turbulence, influenced by rapid shifts in the levels and directions of government spending policy linked to the Vietnam War and the Great Society. Inflation, a comparatively minor problem in the 1940s and 1950s, was approaching double-digit levels and serving as a symptom of deeper challenges within the business sector.

Indianapolis employers felt the changes in many ways. The new youth culture provided both an increased pool of potential workers and a source of potential customers. But the skill levels and the consumer choices required of those workers proved troubling. Nowhere was the problem more immediate than in the entry-level occupations available in the city.

Educational Initiatives

Chamber studies suggested that local employers increasingly required higher educational and vocational skills, leaving less opportunity for the unskilled manual laborer in the local labor force. Yet leaders repeatedly voiced concern that potential workers, whether trained locally or not, often lacked the needed levels of skill. One 1971 study, for example, highlighted the fact that a third of the local labor force lacked even a high school diploma. The result was significant Chamber action for education.

The Chamber continued its practice of working in cooperation with the Indianapolis Public School (IPS) system. Chamber resources were often used to publicize programs of quality in the schools. In particular,

BOARD CHAIR

John Burkhart, 1961-62
Charles E. Wagner, 1963-64

David Rubins, a faculty member of Herron School of Art, shapes "Young Lincoln," which now graces the lawn of the Indiana State House.

INDIANAPOLIS
CHAMBER
OF COMMERCE

The Chamber adopted a new logo in the 1970s.

Capt. Wallace Courtney, a member of the downtown Kiwanis Club, stresses the importance of math and science skills as he demonstrates rocket technology to students from Harshman Junior High School. The visit was among the many activities of the Chamber's Partners In Education program.

the Chamber emphasized the need for adult education and actively encouraged enrollment in IPS evening offerings.

Teacher development continued to enjoy support, although the sheer size of the IPS staff had overwhelmed the earlier program of business visitation. As a more manageable alternative, the Chamber created the Community Resource Workshops in cooperation with local colleges. Each workshop provided eight-week summer study opportunities. The courses focused on the development of classroom aids that would place both national business conditions and local resources in perspective.

The Chamber's long-standing interest in school curriculum was joined by a renewed concern for school management. Although part of this was a desire to provide stability in a time of rapid demographic change, much of it was intended to help the system effectively use scarce tax resources. Typical of the Chamber's involvement was its participation in monitoring a 1975 management study and advising the school system on implementing the study's recommendations for reorganizing administrative support systems in IPS.

The emerging Indiana/Purdue regional campus in Indianapolis, commonly referred to as IUPUI, contained long-existing schools of law, medicine, dentistry, and art. The Chamber enthusiastically supported efforts to expand public higher education in the city while reflecting caution on the question of regional campus autonomy. Chamber Executive Committee minutes reaffirmed that "Chamber policy will take the middle ground between immediate autonomy and a continued relationship with Indiana University and Purdue University."

The Chamber's particular interest was in the creation of an Indianapolis Center for Advanced Research (ICFAR), to look at biomedical and environmental issues. The Center was a long-standing Chamber objective that came to fruition in 1973. It offered counsel in the evolving sciences, incorporating the findings of space-age technology.

Hand in hand with formal education went the Chamber's continuing interest in extracurricular and adult programs. For high school students, the key new program was Opportunities L. A. B. (Learn About Business), a series of ten-day workshops at Wabash College featuring lectures, tours, and simulations of business situations. O.L.A.B. enrolled eighty selected students per session. Students would tour corporations, develop an actual product, design marketing and advertising programs, and liquidate their assets in the end. One group of graduates of the program played turnabout and organized a similar program for their teachers.

New Industries—New Jobs

Education was often linked in Chamber thinking to a fundamental shift in the economic base of the city. Indianapolis, like the Chamber, had traditionally focused its greatest economic interest on manufacturing. But

Members of the Chamber's Job Opportunity Days program for high school seniors helped students set up more than 1,700 interviews with fifty-five businesses in the late 1960s.

Finding jobs for returning
Vietnam War veterans
was an Indianapolis Chamber
concern in 1971.

many aspects of manufacturing were now clearly in decline. This was the period that witnessed the end of meat packing as a major local industry, and that saw such traditionally strong employers as Chrysler and Western Electric planning to curtail or close major facilities.

To offset this proportionate decline in the employment base of the city, many saw opportunities in retailing, wholesaling, and service—and in the related areas of construction and real estate that are often summarized in the term *development*. This shift greatly increased the total number of employers in the area, encouraged the rise of small businesses, and changed the skills and training that many potential employers expected of the local work force.

To publicize these changes and to offer opportunities for employers to meet and recruit potential workers, the Chamber introduced the Job Opportunity Fair in 1966. Although hiring fairs are an old concept in business, no major American city had ever implemented one on the scale that the Chamber was now to devise.

The event was held on a September weekend at the Manufacturer's Building of the Indiana State Fairgrounds. Roughly a hundred employers, representing both the public and private sectors, moved their personnel offices to the site for the weekend. There they scheduled over 2,000 interviews, which resulted in the hiring of at least 556 local workers, three-quarters of whom were unemployed at the time the fair was held.

Such large numbers of participants were, in part, a result of an intensive public relations campaign that began in the summer. A letter was sent to the parents of every one of the 70,000 students in the IPS system. Special letters were sent to all graduating seniors and all night school students in the city. Any interested job applicant was invited to attend special interview technique clinics conducted under the auspices of the Chamber's Committee for Employment Equality. Red Cross volunteers provided free baby-sitting; Yellow Page Girls from Indiana Bell acted as hostesses. Several advisory committees sought to attract groups and individuals who were particularly threatened by unemployment, especially in the minority community. The usual forms of media publicity were joined by a job fair caravan that passed through the streets the week before, led by the Delvados, a popular local singing group.

The Chamber conducted similar job fairs in subsequent years. Eventually these activities were absorbed into other more focused events such as the Chamber's 1968 program for high school seniors, Job Opportunity Days. The special needs of the returning Vietnam veteran were soon recognized, and by 1971 the program was retitled Jobs for Vets and Youth Opportunity Days. Chamber members were encouraged to show their support of these initiatives by displaying a special logo on their company doors.

Another parallel program called Native Son sought to woo the college graduate. Beginning with the Christmas vacation of 1965, the Chamber

A boom in retail development and suburban business expansion brought more employers to the area in the mid 1960s. Lafayette Square, one of the first major malls in this area, was built in 1968.

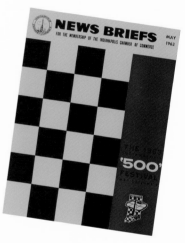

News Briefs continued to be the Chamber's official publication through the early 1960s.

Committee for employment opportunity

Promoting equal opportunity for blacks and other minority groups, the Chamber's Committee for Equal Opportunity encouraged the use of this emblem to hundreds of Indianapolis area employers during the 1960s.

Among high-rises and interstates, some visions of the past remained as the city underwent urban renewal in the 1970s. Built in 1863 at 324 North Park Avenue (Lockerbie Square) by George Holler, this home was restored in 1975 by the Historic Landmarks Foundation of Indiana. It was used as the city's bicentennial celebration headquarters, then sold to a private owner in 1977.

arranged job interviews for college seniors home on vacation. Apart from the desire to find talented workers, the program was specifically designed to encourage local youth to remain within the metropolitan area. In recognition of the growing role of women in the labor force, the name was subsequently changed to Exploration-Graduation. Figures for 1969 are typical of its size and accomplishment: forty-five local businesses conducted approximately 1,200 interviews resulting in the hiring of over 240 college graduates. *The Wall Street Journal* called the program "the most outstanding program in about sixty cities."

The Unemployment Challenge

The problems of the disadvantaged and the hard-core unemployed were of particular concern. The Chamber was convinced that, to be successful, any program of this type must go where the unemployed lived. To that end, a neighborhood recruitment effort was designed. Three neighborhood service centers were designated as sites where the unemployed could receive general information about available jobs, counseling about interview techniques, assistance in completing application forms, and actual job interviews. Staff at the centers would identify individuals in need of employment; the Chamber staff would then strive to match the individuals to job openings listed by local companies. The program succeeded in placing approximately half of those interviewed. Success soon produced a growing caseload that strained the limited staff resources and led to a search for alternative programs.

The most important of these alternatives became the Voluntary Adviser Corps. Initially 300 and later almost 1,000 local businessmen were recruited. Each became a personal adviser to an unemployed worker. The volunteers received training in both counseling techniques and job search methods and were expected to meet and work with individuals who requested assistance. The Chamber was particularly proud of the 85 percent success rate in job placement that resulted over the next few years. Carl Dortch reported to the Lilly Endowment in 1967 that it "demonstrate(s) in Indianapolis the power of the private and independent sector in solving chronic unemployment problems (based on) the concept of identification, referral, evaluation, job listing, and training of the hard-core unemployed."

New Approaches to Housing

These interests in job placement were tied to the Chamber's continuing concern to create a community that would be attractive to both old and new businesses. High on the agenda, as it had been for many years, was the housing question and the related topic of federal funding. The Chamber continued to seek private solutions to the problem.

A survey of low-cost housing was taken in 1967 to see if a privately sponsored pilot project of housing rehabilitation was feasible in the Old

News Briefs, the Chamber's long-standing newsletter, became a full-fledged city magazine with its introduction as *Greater Indianapolis* during the 1960s. At the same time, the Chamber continued to publish a membership directory throughout the business community to encourage area-wide commerce.

Charles E. Wagner, board chair from 1963 to 1964, said in retrospect:

The subject of Civil Rights was very close to the boiling point all over the country during my term. The good people of Indianapolis had, for many years, labored to make ours a good community for all our people, and we were anxious to continue to progress without becoming victims of the hysteria which brought such heartbreaks elsewhere. Many discussions took place with . . . leaders of the Negro citizenry, a series of meetings was held for the purpose of helping qualified workers to find jobs. In short, every move was directed toward helping colored people to help themselves.

Fireworks lit up the night sky as the Claypool Hotel marked its final evening of existence. The Bates House, founding site of today's Indianapolis Chamber, was demolished the next day.

Northside area just south of Fall Creek. Four local banks participated in the rehabilitation of five houses as a test of private initiative.

The banks, however, declined to participate in an expanded program involving 225 residences in the area bounded by Talbot, Sixteenth, College, and Twenty-Second Streets. Instead, a separate corporation, Indianapolis Neighborhood Housing, Inc., was formed in 1969 to rehabilitate 225 units and build 75 new units in a series of stages. The project was funded by a $2.7 million mortgage commitment from New York Life and supported by a 25 percent guarantee from Lilly Endowment. Two primary contractors and a number of subcontractors, including minority businesses, became involved. Progress was steady but disappointingly slow. In the first year, 230 workers were hired and 26 residences completed and occupied by local residents. Ultimately, 137 units were completed before the project was halted by a combination of vandalism, delays, and inadequate performance by some of the subcontractors.

The limited success of the project, and especially the inability to draw local banks more fully into the enterprise, caused the Chamber to rethink its position on federal funding and to adopt a new policy statement. In 1967 the Chamber expressed its position: "An amendment of philosophy is needed in funding the needs of local development. [We] seek a method to make use of federal funds as long as control remains in the hands of local communities."

The Unigov Era

Such a search necessarily involved local government, which was itself going through a major reorganization. The reorganization involved the consolidation of a number of functions previously performed by separate civil agencies of city government, county government, and certain city-county commissions, into a new county-wide metropolitan government commonly called Unigov. The consolidation was not all-encompassing, because it did not touch upon police and fire services or upon the school systems. But in a number of areas, such as administration and transportation, it marked the most significant reorganization of government since the city charter of 1892.

The Chamber strongly supported Unigov. Carl Dortch represented the Chamber on the citizen committee that laid plans for the change, and Chamber members and officers regularly testified in support of the idea. Unigov was seen as an extension of the long-established Chamber attempts to link the development of the suburbs to the life of the older city, provide a more comprehensive planning function, and obtain an adequate tax base for many urban and suburban services. In a state without home rule, Unigov required the action of the General Assembly, where the Chamber was an enthusiastic advocate of the change. It also required action by the courts to approve the legislation, and here the Chamber initiated the necessary lawsuit to assist the Unigov proponents.

Roy Echols, board chair from 1965 to 1966, dedicated the Chamber's seventy-fifth anniversary celebration in these words:

We look backwards with pride and forward with confidence. A backward look reveals a one-man staff 75 years ago occupying a cubby hole office and serving about 1,000 members in a city just beginning to sense its destiny. Through the years, aided by the diligent efforts of thousands of men, we grew with Indianapolis and helped it to grow. Today we comprise an organization of 25 full-time specialists, plus 500 volunteers serving on committees, with a total membership support of more than 5,100 in this city on the verge of greatness . . . We shall succeed!

Marti Waltz plays "music to demolish by" during the demolition of the eleven-story Knights of Pythias building at the intersection of Ohio, Delaware, Pennsylvania, and New York Streets to make way for the thirty-seven story INB building on June 9, 1967.

The 4,000-acre Eagle Creek Park on the city's northwest side provides a haven for urban and rural dwellers alike. Eagle Creek Park sets aside several tracts within the park as wildlife preserves.

The newly consolidated city-county government soon became an active partner in many of the urban initiatives being proposed at the time. Under Mayor Richard Lugar, Unigov assumed many of the programs in public housing, job recruitment, and federal funding that had long absorbed local attention. Even more, Unigov became a partner in downtown redevelopment.

Rejuvenating Downtown Indianapolis

In 1966 the Chamber commissioned a survey of the city's center, called the Mile Square, to review its current condition and future prospects. The report proved disturbing. It found retail store sales had declined 31 percent in constant dollars in the period from 1948 to 1963: "Perhaps no downtown business district in the nation has suffered so drastic an actual and relative decline in its retailing function as has downtown Indianapolis since the end of World War II. In 1948 the percentage of total retail sales in the central business district was 87%, in 1963 it was 46.1%. . . . The downtown is still uninviting, uninspiring, and basically inefficient as the commercial nerve center of a large metropolitan area."

On the other hand, the report was designed to focus attention on the prospects for improvement. It highlighted the positive features that could become the basis of downtown revitalization. These included a sound approach to industrial planning that could be applied in the retail district and the possibility of government involvement: "Problems of downtown are those of obsolescence, congestion, and inaccessibility. Each . . . is amenable to solution through concerted public and private efforts. . . . The missing ingredient is integrated programming and planning in a joint public and private approach."

A second report financed by the Department of Housing and Urban Development in 1969 amplified upon the possibilities of change and success. It found that

Indianapolis is at a take-off point in development. Its structure of urban services has broadened and deepened to the point of critical mass, where each new addition to the package would induce something else to happen. (The city's) secret weapon continues to be its skill at running a first-class city. Of all major U.S. cities in which strategies for action might be suggested from the outside, Indianapolis is the area for which the process might be least justified. It is not a matter of local receptivity; it is rather one of local competence. Indianapolis is America's number one do-it-yourself city, which bespeaks a high degree of local sensitivity, responsibility, and performance.

The "Indianapol**IS**" Campaign

Such surveys, combined with their recent experiences in housing, led Chamber leaders to conclude that the most important action they could

Indianapolis played host to the International Conference on Cities in 1970.

Look magazine proclaimed Indianapolis an All-American City in 1971. The accompanying article praised the city for its "belief in private effort for public needs," citing such features as:
• the first public television station established by citizen action, as 9,000 women volunteers raised $300,000 in the opening campaign;
• a Metropolitan Manpower Commission of volunteer businessmen that located 24,000 jobs for local workers in its first two years; and,
• the Unigov program that succeeded in simultaneously improving services and lowering taxes.

Carl Dortch, president of the Indianapolis Chamber from 1964 to 1979, shakes hands with Mayor John Barton at the kickoff of the petition campaign for the Eagle Creek Reservoir and Park in 1964.

115

Market Square Arena saw Indianapolis revitalization at its peak during the 1970s, coinciding with the Chamber's promotion nationwide of the "IndianapolIS" campaign. "IndianapolIS" promoted economic development to new heights.

116

take would be to attract new investors to the city. A 1971 survey helped to highlight features in the community attractive to such investment. It led to the "Indianapol**IS**" campaign of 1973.

The campaign's kickoff brochure proclaimed it was designed to "build a diversified economic base, enhance the quality of life . . . , and focus national attention upon Indianapolis as one of America's greatest cities."

The campaign reflected the Chamber's traditional emphasis upon organized promotion of new business, equitable taxation, and the quality of community life. Cooperation with local government and the quest for improved transportation continued to be important ideas. Carefully planned, the campaign sought to involve the full Chamber membership in a wide variety of promotional activities. Many of these incorporated extensive volunteer service on task forces and in community organizations which were seen as partners of the Chamber.

Among the most visible of the changes advocated were a Small Business Council that conducted short courses on management, a state property tax relief law passed with Chamber support, and the creation of a Metropolitan Arts Council. A series of task forces which paralleled the departments of city-county government advised on the budgeting process, and a major expansion of the airport into an international facility was successfully initiated.

The Chamber's Changing Face

The varied activities of "Indianapol**IS**," and more generally the changes in the city since 1965, pointed up the changing face of the Chamber itself. In these years the transition away from industry in the city was reflected in a new diversity in the membership and leadership of the Chamber.

As with most modern voluntary associations, the Chamber had adopted the distinction between a board responsible for establishing policy and a staff responsible for its implementation. Board officers, headed by an annually elected chairman, reflected the business leadership of the city, both in owners of local firms and in managers of local segments of national corporations. Drawn from real estate, construction, and small business, board leaders were indicative of a changing community; programs such as a pilot attempt to provide group health insurance to small businesses were suggestive of the different needs of newer members.

The staff, now headed by a president, had grown in size and in the specialization of its functions, outgrowing its old offices and preparing for the move to the upper floors of the Chamber building. The key staff figure at this time was Carl Dortch, who had joined the Chamber in the summer of 1935 and who had assumed the presidency in the mid-1960s. Dortch brought both continuity and an unassuming mastery of fact and statistical detail to the Chamber. He assumed a central role in the city's decision-making process, providing a personal link between business, govern-

The Chamber regularly sponsored Chamber Night at Bush Stadium. Here, a likely group of attendees pose at Bat Day in 1966 to see the Indianapolis Indians.

The successful Chamber program, "IndianapolIS," kicked off in 1973, had a mission to "stimulate growth and focus national attention on Indianapolis as one of America's greatest cities."

Indianapolis Magazine was published by the Indianapolis Chamber until 1983 when it was sold to an outside agent. The publication was Indianapolis' only general interest city magazine for many years. It ceased publication in 1989.

Fourth of July festivities downtown
have become an Indianapolis
tradition.

ment, and the voluntary sector that touched subjects as varied as park development, sewer construction, and tax legislation.

The most evident feature of the changes in the Chamber was the need to reassess its financial base. Membership dues from its traditional members were only providing about a third of the total funds that moved through the Chamber budget. Increasingly its projects were funded by grant support given by local foundations, by special project-oriented fund drives, and by various in-kind services and donations. Several of the changes in direction of individual projects were directly traceable to the presence, or absence, of special funds. At least one project, the Voluntary Adviser Corps, needed to be transferred to city government when private sources proved inadequate.

The solution which the Chamber adopted was to expand its membership base and raise its dues levels. Success in both required evidence of activity on the Chamber's part; the "Indianapol**IS**" project went far to move the Chamber in this direction. So, too, did new actions designed to involve a growing number of individuals in the workings of the Chamber. In 1966 a Council of Past Presidents was created, and in 1974 a Society of Retired Executives was begun. Then, in 1976, Edna Lacy's support permitted the Chamber to organize the Stanley K. Lacy Executive Leadership Series to give young leaders an introduction to the business and civic community.

By the middle 1970s the Chamber was thus positioned to become a much more inclusive organization than before and was looking actively in new directions. Both approaches would be achieved in the years to come.

The Stanley K. Lacy Executive Leadership Series was created in 1976 under the direction of Edna Lacy. The program educates twenty-five young leaders each year and prepares them to take the lead in community service programs and projects.

Bob Eaglesfield, a volunteer from the Society of Retired Executives, discussed uses of energy to fifth and sixth grade honor roll students in the science club at Edgar H. Evans School #11. The Society of Retired Executives, an affiliate program of the Chamber, was organized in 1974 and enlists the services of retired professionals to provide voluntary technical and advisory help to community, educational, and business organizations.

Chapter 7

Into The Future

Major changes in Indianapolis in the 1970s and 1980s were mirrored in the Chamber of Commerce. Expanded membership and membership activities, a more democratic and voluntaristic approach to leadership, collaborative partnerships with varied civic organizations, and active support for the urban renaissance kept the Chamber in the mainstream of local affairs.

The Context—Public Opinion

As the voice of the Indianapolis business community, the Chamber was often influenced by public perceptions of business. Local Chamber leaders were much impressed by studies conducted in the 1970s by the nationally regarded market opinion research firm of Yankelovich, Skelly, and White.

The studies suggested that dramatic changes had occurred in the public's attitudes toward the enterprise system. Traditional critics of business had been joined by many who were once favorable to its position. Overall positive ratings of the business community had fallen as low as 19 percent nationally. In particular, concern over product safety and health, apparent profiteering by the oil industry, and the general suspicion of leadership following the Watergate crisis had contributed to the decline. The public, the survey showed, did not believe that profits were any longer a reward for service, but were instead a result of gouging and profiteering. In such a climate of opinion, it was important that business work to regain public confidence.

Partners for Jobs

The studies reinforced two related Chamber beliefs: belief in the need to show an active interest in the larger good of the local community, and belief in the need to work in partnership with other civic institutions. As Thomas Binford, Chamber board chairman from 1983 to 1984, summarized the approach, "It was necessary to extend the benefits of the free enterprise system to everyone in the community."

Jobs lay at the heart of this response; youth employment lay at the heart of the jobs issue; black youths were the primary target group. In 1977 the Chamber's Urban Affairs Council approached city government and expressed concern that 110 separate agencies were working on the problem. The council proposed the Indianapolis Business Alliance for Jobs to provide the necessary central coordination.

Opposite: After facing the same urban decay that befell other cities in the 1960s, Indianapolis underwent a major downtown renaissance in the 1970s with nearly $4 million in both public and private money invested or committed to downtown projects from 1974 to 1990.

Carl Dortch (standing), who became president of the Chamber in 1964, handed over the office of leadership in 1979 to Thomas King, who led the organization into its 100th year in 1990.

The Changing Face of the Membership

By 1987, membership in the Indianapolis Chamber was more than 85 percent small business and mirrored the local business community in diversity by business sector.

Partners In Education took many forms. Through Arsenal Technical High School, it has led since 1980 to an award-winning set of homes built on the Old Northside and the Near Eastside by the Career Education Center Builders, Inc. The PIE program has offered students the opportunity to learn the building trades in partnership with volunteer builders, architects, attorneys, and other professionals. Above, Chuck Nelson, a 1988 graduate of Arsenal Tech, poses with Mayor William Hudnut, III, on June 2, 1988 in dedicating an addition to the neighborhood at 1500 Central Avenue. Nelson and his peers built the fifth of a six-home micro/neighborhood located on the Old Northside. The program has led many students, like Nelson, to careers in the construction trades.

The Alliance was quickly at work, sponsoring several programs. First among these was Hire a Youth, designed to place youths aged sixteen to twenty-one in small business jobs. Next was the Volunteer Alliance, a renewal of the Chamber's earlier attempt to provide one-on-one counseling to the unemployed. In conjunction with the National Alliance for Business, the local Alliance also conducted an annual Jobs Campaign. This identified job opportunities in the private sector and promoted hiring the disadvantaged. The Chamber employed ninety-eight disadvantaged youths in 1978, placing them in the Vocational Exploration Program.

Jobs for veterans continued to be a special Chamber interest. In cooperation with the city government, the Chamber conducted H. I. R. E. (Help through Industry Retraining Employment). Employers could be reimbursed for up to half the expense of hiring and retraining a veteran. Up to ninety trainees at a time moved through the system.

The Chamber next helped to organize and support Partners 2000, which functioned as a summer youth employment program. Working in support of JobNet, a network of several hundred business volunteers combed the city each spring asking "Just For Jobs." In 1983 the goal was 1,000 private sector jobs for youth. By 1987, 2,400 youths a year were placed. As the name suggested, Partners 2000 was a collaborative effort, involving not only the Chamber, but also the Greater Indianapolis Progress Committee and a number of sponsoring local businesses.

Partners for Education

The Chamber also continued its educational initiatives in partnership with the Indianapolis Public Schools. Many of these activities were tied to two significant changes in the schools: a court-mandated desegregation of the IPS system and the reduction in facilities and teachers occasioned by the decline in the postwar baby boom. The Chamber generally worked with the school board, even supporting an unsuccessful 1985 referendum to raise the property tax for school support. The Chamber was also a public supporter of peaceful desegregation and an active participant in the program to assist teachers who were laid off. Most important among the joint efforts of the Chamber and IPS was the 1979 creation of Partners In Education, which encouraged and nurtured mutually beneficial partnerships between individual businesses and schools in the IPS system.

Partners was originally conceived as a program for the high schools, but it soon grew to include almost every school in IPS, and even several township schools. Each business sponsor was charged to create one or more programs that would assist its school by involving students in projects related to the work of the company. Students thus achieved insight into the workplace while being introduced to potential future career opportunities. By the mid 1980s, the Partners program was a national model, and by 1988, literacy, parent involvement, and school attendance were emerging as new focal points of partnership activity.

Partners 2000, which began in 1983, was a collaborative effort of the Chamber and a number of other organizations to supply summer jobs to local young people. Now administered by the Indianapolis Alliance for Jobs, the program was employing 2,400 youths by 1987.

The Chamber's work in education, which became a priority for the organization as early as the 1900s, was most successful in creating interaction between students and adult role models. Skating star Tai Babalonia was among the celebrities to address students through the Chamber's Partners In Education program.

Fifth graders from Lewis W. Gilfoy School #113 learn how sonobuoys work in detecting submarines deep beneath the ocean surface from David Hollenberger, an electronics engineer with Naval Avionics.

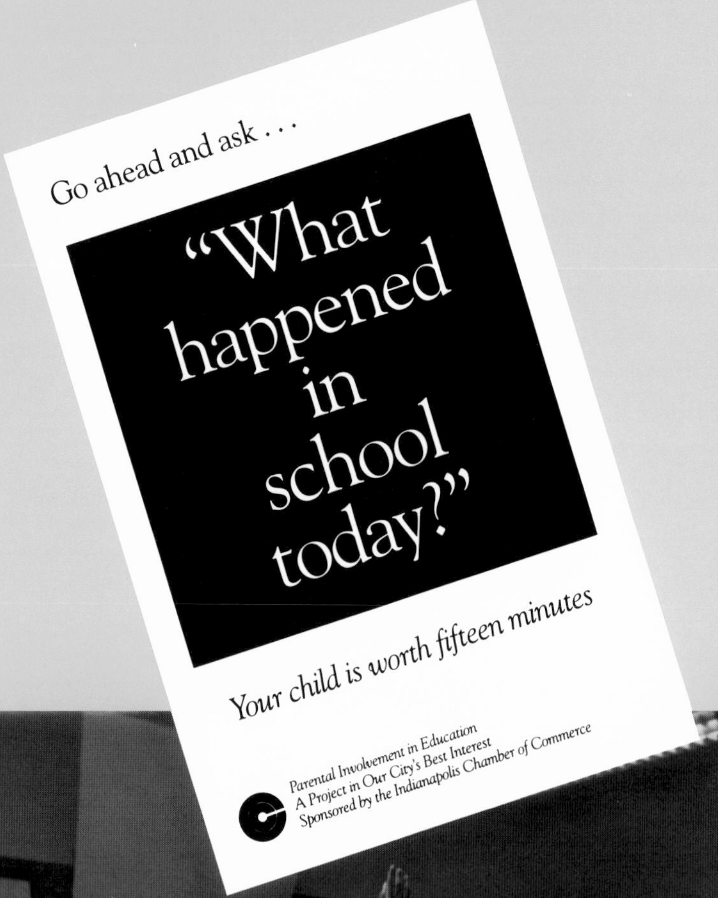

Go ahead and ask . . .

"What
happened
in
school
today?"

Your child is worth fifteen minutes

Parental Involvement in Education
A Project in Our City's Best Interest
Sponsored by the Indianapolis Chamber of Commerce

Responding to the times once
again, the Chamber addressed the
need for parent involvement in
education in 1989 by challenging
working parents to ask "What
happened in school today?" The
message reached thousands of
working parents through an
instructional video, payroll
stuffers, and training workshops.

A Winning Team project to boost attendance matched each school with a coach recruited from among community leaders, government officials, and sports and media personalities. Mayor William Hudnut, III, Marion County Prosecutor Steve Goldsmith, and popular Indianapolis Indians first baseman "Razor" Shines were among those offering positive role models and personal encouragement to students—and obtaining positive results.

In the late 1980s, awareness efforts were directed at parent involvement. Using the slogan "Your Child is Worth 15 Minutes," the Chamber promoted parent training workshops and used an instructional video and payroll check stuffers as part of a major media campaign. Parents were encouraged to ask "What happened in school today?" as a stepping stone to involvement in their children's education. The Chamber also began to investigate the problems of adult literacy, seeking ways to assist the adult as well as the youth labor force.

The Partners program also provided students opportunities to gain construction trade skills through Career Education Center Builders, Inc., a cooperative effort between the Chamber, IPS, Eastside Community Investments, and the Builders Association of Greater Indianapolis.

Partners in the Community

Collaboration extended to other community interests. The Chamber regularly functioned as a clearinghouse to identify and match potential volunteers with interested civic organizations. Part of this effort fell within the continuing Stanley K. Lacy series; part was conducted at the staff level in the Chamber offices. In 1981, *The Indianapolis Star* praised the "Chamber's community work, providing staff and services" to numerous community activities.

This effort also took advantage of overlapping membership on boards of directors, a circumstance that is common in Indianapolis. Chamber presidents, directors, and officers were often found on other governing bodies such as the White River Park Commission, the Pan-Am Task Force on Housing, and the PAX/I Chamber Community Partners Business Initiative.

In the same period, the Chamber's Women's Council —descendent of the groups first formed when women were admitted in the 1920s—dissolved its traditional recognition banquet and redirected its efforts to the promotion of volunteerism by members. The council focused on local cultural agencies, especially the new Indianapolis Museum of Art, and abandoned its separate organization to become a Business and Professional Women's Division. The members' volunteer work enabled the museum to expand its hours.

The Chamber's heightened sense of business' social responsibility led to the creation of The 2%-5% Club in 1985 for firms contributing between 2 and 5 percent of their pre-tax profits to community organiza-

Noting a trend in declining attendance among junior high school students, the Chamber created The Winning Team, using community leaders as "coaches" to inspire and encourage improvement. The program achieved positive results.

The compilation of economic statistics and market data continued to be the Chamber's primary work in the 1980s just as it had been during the early years of the Commercial Club.

At the urging of Mayor William Hudnut, III, the Indianapolis Chamber studied the feasibility of an expanded convention center and domed stadium in 1977 with positive results.

tions, philanthropic projects, or religious, educational, and civic causes. They were invited to do so at a time when the national average for such contributions was just over 1 percent. The charter membership was eighty-six, and the total, contrary to the usual pattern of such groups, increased each year thereafter.

A Livable Community

These activities meshed well with the Chamber's traditional emphasis on an attractive and livable community. A good example was its continuing involvement with the Indiana Convention Center. The Center itself had opened in the late 1960s, spurred by downtown development, a state law permitting Sunday liquor sales, and active fund-raising by a Chamber committee led by Roy Echols, board chairman from 1965 to 1966.

By 1977 the city government was seeking to expand the Center and to add a major domed stadium, ultimately to be named the Hoosier Dome, and the potential scope and expense of the project had raised local concern. At the mayor's urging, the Chamber undertook a feasibility study that reaffirmed the potential success of the expansion. As Mayor Hudnut later noted, "It all started when we asked the Chamber Executive Committee to support us in a study of the . . . desirability of the project." The Chamber also determined funding strategies and led a lobbying effort to secure that funding.

The Chamber continued to show its interest in attracting sports teams and events to the city. Chamber representatives were active on committees or task forces concerned with securing an NFL football franchise, a downtown facility for the National Clay Courts competition, and a stadium to host a major league baseball team.

Visible Achievements

Viewed from the Chamber's offices, the growth of Indianapolis as a major center for both professional and amateur sports fitted well within the continuing "IndianapolIS" campaign. By 1979 a Chamber study concluded that the city had developed a positive image among both current and prospective residents. The study also cautioned that major demographic shifts continued to pose challenges for city and county business people. Chief among the challenges was the projected rapid growth of population and the ensuing shift of retail business to the surrounding counties.

The final review of the "IndianapolIS" campaign highlighted the record of continued success. It noted that since 1973 the city had attracted more than thirty major new businesses each year, had accounted for a total investment in new and expanded facilities of about $325 million, and had seen at least 2,700 new jobs created.

Encouraged by such successes, the Chamber launched a subsequent promotional campaign in 1981 in cooperation with the Greater Indian-

Eugene B. Hibbs, 1977-78
Alex S. Carroll, 1979-80

Thomas W. Moses, 1981-82

In the midst of Indianapolis' emergence as an amateur sports capital, the Chamber's Corporate Challenge pitted corporate teams against each other in friendly competition. The annual fall event has since become one of the organization's most visible attractions.

Sen. Richard Lugar was among the participants in 1985.

127

Following in the footsteps of past trade shows and capitalizing on the success of smaller shows like Buy Greater Indianapolis First, the Chamber answered member demand for greater visibility in 1988 to create Chamber Expo, which hosted nearly 300 displayers to an audience of over 8,000 patrons. Above, restauranteer Mike Flanagan discusses business with a fellow member at a 1986 Buy Greater Indianapolis First at the Hilton Hotel on the Circle.

apolis Progress Committee. As a measure of the sophistication and new technology of the decade, the new campaign featured targeted direct mailings to potential investors, a multimedia tape presentation, and three "Visit Indianapolis" events planned for interested prospects. The campaign placed heavy emphasis upon the revitalization of downtown, the theme of partnership, and the favorable business climate that resulted.

Partners for Business

The "Visit Indianapolis" campaign also served to highlight the increased difficulty of conducting traditional economic development. The Chamber continued to welcome basic industrial expansion and to engage in the type of scientific promotion so familiar throughout its history. But the group now began to focus more intently upon active solicitation of new or expanded businesses.

In the process, the Chamber sometimes worked in partnership with the Indianapolis Convention and Visitors Bureau. They were operating on the assumption that the many conventions that visited the city offered the opportunity to attract prospects from among the delegates. Projects included a focus upon city tours and colorful promotional brochures.

The Chamber also began a series of well-attended trade shows to offer its members the opportunity for increased visibility. Beginning as Buy Greater Indianapolis First, the shows were held in local hotel lobbies with over 100 displayers. By 1988 the demand for space prompted a move to the Indiana Convention Center for the creation of the Chamber Expo, a new show boasting over 300 displayers and attendance by over 8,000.

Partners, and Problems, with Government

A major continuing activity of the Chamber was its relationship with government and with public questions affecting business. The Chamber continued to be actively involved with the Indiana General Assembly. The traditional role of representing its members before government was given renewed emphasis in the mid-1980s when the Chamber continued its practice of offering policy and position papers on issues before the legislature.

Some of its interests were ongoing, notably concern for Indiana taxes. The inventory tax, levied each spring upon the value of a firm's inventory, was both a cause of endless inventory reduction sales and a continuing annoyance to many Chamber members. It proved, as always, to be a difficult issue for the Chamber. There was united opposition to the tax, but there was no united view of an alternative source of state revenue. Unable to agree fully upon the alternative, the Chamber continued to concentrate upon alerting legislators to the effect of the tax upon the business climate. The Chamber also continued to call for the phaseout of the corporate gross receipts tax and for tort reform in state law.

Thomas W. Binford, 1983-84
Phillip R. Duke, 1985-86

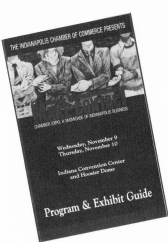

After studying the feasibility and encouraging the expansion of the Indiana Convention Center, Thomas King, Chamber president, and John Myrland, executive vice president, participated in a signing ceremony to permit Sunday liquor sales and officially begin expansion proceedings.

Pictured are: (seated, left to right) Lt. Gov. John Mutz, Gov. Robert Orr, and Mayor William Hudnut, III; (standing, left to right) Myrland, Tom Moses, the Chamber's board chair at the time, King, and Bill Carter, chairman of the Chamber's Stadium Task Force.

Indianapolis' failure to meet clean air standards for the pollutant ozone in 1978 led the Chamber to campaign for "air quality." With the bulk of the problem attributed to auto emissions, the organization began an area-wide public education effort complete with auto testings at local shopping malls.

Chamber president Thomas King and Mayor William Hudnut, III, announce a program to promote public awareness of the pollutant ozone in the summer of 1987.

Other interests reflected the new issues of a changing city. A growing spirit of home rule in the legislature, for example, had been accompanied by a local option sales tax. Concerned about the effect upon retail business in Marion County if the tax were not enacted in neighboring areas, the Chamber opposed the measure and convinced the mayor not to enact it in Marion County. Chamber representatives continued to attend all meetings of the City-County Council, offered advice regarding the city budget, and supported an ambitious project called the Circle Centre Mall. Changes in campaign finance laws led the Chamber to develop its first Political Action Committee in 1978 to give financial support to several state legislative candidates.

The Chamber also found itself involved in a continuing discussion with the Environmental Protection Agency (EPA) over air quality in Indianapolis. The issue was troubling for the Chamber because it pitted two of the organization's major interests against one another. As a group concerned with creating a livable community, the Chamber sought clean air; as a group concerned with business growth and expansion, the Chamber opposed undue federal regulation and intervention.

When the issue first surfaced in 1973, it dealt with the question of auto emission controls. The Chamber noted the unusually high costs involved in the original EPA proposal and expressed concern for the effects of sudden changes in regulations on downtown businesses. In cooperation with the city government, the Chamber worked to revise the plan in ways that would make costs and regulations more manageable. It then spent considerable time monitoring the ensuing agreement. When the U. S. Chamber of Commerce subsequently dealt with the Clean Air Act, it drew heavily upon the successes of the Indianapolis Chamber's approach.

The issue became immediate in 1978 when the city failed to meet EPA air quality standards and came under pressure to impose new regulations. Because this would include stricter building permit standards, the Chamber took an active interest. It organized a vigorous effort that linked intensive lobbying with an innovative environmental management program. A special consultant was hired to advise government units and local businesses on how to develop plans to meet the EPA standards and reporting guidelines.

The major source of local problems was ozone, a pollutant formed when hydrocarbons mix with sunlight. Automobile emissions contributed 55 percent of the ozone levels, threatening an EPA cutoff of highway dollars and a halt to economic development if not checked. The Chamber concentrated much of its efforts on motor vehicle testing and repair as a means of avoiding more stringent regulations. The Chamber took an aggressive stand recommending mandatory inspections as the only real solution to the problem. When this stand encountered political resistance, the Chamber also encouraged voluntary inspections as an interim step, using the slogan "If You Love Your Family, Give Your Car

Frank D. Walker, 1986-88
Andrew J. Paine, Jr., 1989-90

The Chamber's government affairs staff, John Myrland, executive vice president, and Mark Ahearn, department director, discuss the legislative agenda for business and the concern for the city's air quality during a local talk show, mid-1980.

One measure of an organization's success is the volume of its activities. In 1990, on an average day, the Chamber offices on North Meridian Street will

• receive more than 300 telephone calls,

• process nearly 60 requests for information, and

• serve some 20 newcomers and potential new residents.

131

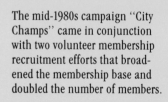

1984 ANNUAL REPORT

CITY CHAMPS

INDIANAPOLIS
CHAMBER
OF COMMERCE

The mid-1980s campaign "City Champs" came in conjunction with two volunteer membership recruitment efforts that broadened the membership base and doubled the number of members.

A Physical." In the late 1980s, testing sites were opened at suburban malls, and educational and media handouts were distributed as part of the campaign.

Internal Growth

Such developments in the external activities of the Chamber were mirrored in internal changes. At the end of 1979, Thomas King succeeded Carl Dortch as president of the Chamber. An experienced member of the staff and an advocate of effective internal services for members, King led the Chamber as it sought to create a more inclusive and involved membership, introduce new management practices and objectives, and expand benefits to members.

The new membership emphasis arose from a 1980 planning study which noted that the Chamber was disproportionately composed of larger business firms. A market survey showed that 61 percent of its businesses had more than 100 employees and 57 percent had between 51 and 100 employees. Only 9 percent of businesses of 50 or fewer employees were Chamber members.

Yet the survey also showed that 95 percent of all local businesses fell into the latter category, leaving the Chamber overall with only 12 percent of its potential market share.

The Chamber therefore decided to broaden its membership base with a series of aggressive recruitment drives. The first began in 1982 and generated over 300 new members in a few weeks. An innovative feature of the drive was a loaned executive program by which local companies designated a staff member to work as a Chamber recruitment officer.

Alongside a highly successful image campaign, "City Champs," a 1986 membership effort was directed at small businesses. The effort recruited more than 800 volunteer solicitors organized into corporate teams on a competitive basis. The solicitors hoped to gain about 500 new members. They actually gained over 1,350. The targeted dues revenue sought was $100,000. The actual amount achieved was $247,000. The campaign, coupled with an equally successful campaign the following year, moved the Chamber from near the bottom in its membership base among comparable cities to the national average for city chambers.

Heightened membership numbers pointed directly to the need for membership services and activities that would maintain that base. Much of the Chamber's internal activities in the 1980s were directed to that goal. King described the Chamber's operations as "market driven, meaning that the Chamber took a hard look at who it serves and the reason it exists. . . . The services that the members most want are networking opportunities that permit them to meet other business leaders."

The Chamber soon began a program of new member receptions hosted by the Board of Directors, and then it followed these with a variety of business seminars. The seminars ranged widely over the challenges

Promotional materials used in support of membership recruitment campaigns during the 1980s called for community-wide support to aid the Chamber mission.

Membership Growth 1978-1990

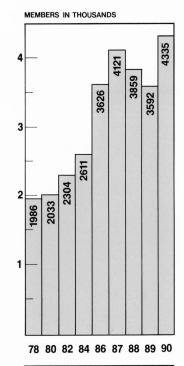

MEMBERS IN THOUSANDS

Year	Members
78	1986
80	2033
82	2304
84	2611
86	3626
87	4121
88	3859
89	3592
90	4335

133

Top: The Indianapolis Chamber celebrated its 100-year legacy of service in 1990 as "The Key to the City for 100 Years."

Bottom: Representatives from the Chamber's only still-existing founding companies join board chairman Andrew Paine, Jr., president of INB National Bank, for a toast at the 1990 annual meeting of the membership. From left to right are Thomas Miller of INB National Bank, Frank Caperton of *The Indianapolis News,* Paine, and Stephen Stitle of Eli Lilly and Company.

facing business in the 1980s. They included dealing with crime, conducting employee evaluations, planning career strategies for women in today's business, starting a new small business, and learning that "What You Are Isn't Necessarily What You Will Be, And What You Are Is Where You See." The number of seminars jumped from six in 1983 to twenty-six in 1985, with a five-fold increase in participation.

The Chamber also sought to give its members more opportunities for volunteer activities in both the Chamber and the community. Committee memberships were expanded to include new members. The board's Nominating Committee sought to name candidates who reflected the new diversity of the membership base. The Opportunity Indianapolis program was initiated, modeled on the Lacy Leadership program. Thirty to thirty-five business leaders at a time participated in a series of meetings designed to acquaint them with a range of community service opportunities while developing their leadership skills.

Small Business Leadership

The Chamber also provided services to its growing number of small business members through a new Small Business Division. Most notable was an affordable new plan that provided group health and life insurance for firms employing fewer than fifty employees. The division worked closely with the affiliated Society of Retired Executives to overcome any difficulties which hindered members from utilizing Chamber resources and services.

A monthly survey of fifty different Chamber members helped the staff determine what services were being used. New members were interviewed to find out what new services were in demand. Some programs were eliminated as not essential to member interests, including the city image and urban affairs programs and the Chamber's publication, *Indianapolis Magazine*. New approaches recognized the importance of the small business community. In 1988, for example, the *Small Business Clearinghouse* was created, and a special emphasis was placed on increasing the number of minority business owners and entrepreneurs.

Throughout, the emphasis was upon an inclusive attitude toward community business: "The Chamber represents all its members, regardless of location within the service area. Therefore, regional favoritism is to be avoided."

The changes, as King noted, put the Chamber on the "cutting edge of Chamber activities nationwide"—where it has so often been in its one hundred years of service. The changes also confirmed the Chamber's ability to participate in a variety of key roles in the urban vitality of Indianapolis. By linking the business community to the other participants in the process, the Chamber continued to perform well the functions for which it had been created a century before.

At its opening meeting in 1890, the Commercial Club of Indianapolis declared its purpose "to promote the prosperity and work for the general welfare of Indianapolis." The statement was soon refined to "promotion of the commercial and manufacturing interests and the general welfare of the City of Indianapolis, Marion County, Indiana and vicinity."

One hundred years later, the Indianapolis Chamber's mission remains essentially the same: "To influence the development of the greater Indianapolis area for the purpose of maintaining a favorable business climate and creating economic growth. The mission will be accomplished on behalf of the business community, particularly Chamber members, by providing direct services, by representing members on matters that affect them, and by directing member resources toward community issues that are of importance to them."

In 1989, the Chamber embraced the philosophy of quality to ensure excellent customer service: "As the staff of the Indianapolis Chamber of Commerce, our quality mission is to provide products and services that anticipate, meet or exceed the needs and expectations of our internal and external customers. In pursuit of this quality mission, each of us is committed to teamwork, pride in excellence, continual improvement, and an ongoing process of evaluation and assessment."

Conclusion

The Indianapolis Chamber of Commerce of 1990 is very different from the Commercial Club that had formed at the Bates House a century before. An original membership of twenty-seven has grown to over 4,000, company memberships have replaced individual stockholders, and a staff of one has grown to more than thirty.

Different also are many of the specific issues which the Chamber addresses. Track elevation and street paving have yielded to open housing, interstate highway routes, clean air, and suburban development. A focus upon manufacturing, while never abandoned, has been joined by interests in retail, wholesale, and development activities. The Chamber is a much bigger and more varied organization, as is the city of which it is a part.

Indianapolis remains in 1990 one of the major urban centers of the country, ranking fourteenth in population and thirty-fifth among metropolitan areas. Its success and its distinctive features owe much to the Chamber. On issues as varied as education, housing, transportation, public health, safety, and taxation, Indianapolis has been influenced by the ideas and by the programs put forth by the Chamber of Commerce. And in the economic sphere, there is little question that the Chamber's emphasis upon research, scientific promotion, fair taxation, job creation, and community cooperation have made major contributions to the city's growth and development.

As former board chairman Boris Meditch notes, "the Chamber is most effective in bringing various segments of the community together that have differences and misunderstandings. . . . Its strength is in its strong leadership at the volunteer level, backed up by a very professional staff." And as Chamber president Tom King summarizes its work, "It's not wise to try to promote our way to success. We must take the long-range view, remember what's been done, and be mindful of the basics that need improving."

Within the context of great change, the Indianapolis Chamber of Commerce shows great continuity. From its founding to the present day, it has sought to be the voice of business in the city and has spoken with consistency on issue after issue. Its underlying approach has changed little from that articulated by Colonel Lilly a century ago. Under many leaders, it has sought to encourage "Indianapolis First."

Partners In Progress

The Associated Group

Baker & Daniels

BANK ONE,
INDIANAPOLIS, NA

Barnes & Thornburg

Business
Furniture
Corporation

Citizens
Gas & Coke
Utility

Community
Hospitals Indianapolis

Ice Miller
Donadio and Ryan

INB National Bank

The Indianapolis News

Indianapolis
Power & Light
Company

Jenn-Air Company

Lacy Diversified
Industries, Ltd.

Eli Lilly and Company

Marsh Supermarkets

Merchants
National Bank
and Trust Company

Park Fletcher, Inc.

Railroadmen's
Federal Savings &
Loan Association

Ransburg Corporation

St. Francis
Hospital Center

St. Vincent Hospital
and Health Care Center

Union Federal
Savings Bank

Walker Research, Inc.

Indiana
Historical Society

One hundred years ago, Eli Lilly, Indiana National, the News, Kiefer Stewart, and Van Camp Hardware and Iron were among the prominent business partners to Indianapolis. The following are among our partners in progress today.

137

The Associated Group

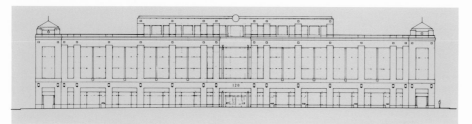

Next home: An architect's drawing of The Associated Group's new headquarters, 120 Monument Circle, opening early in 1991.

Today: A sense of mission

Two companies that began modestly in the 1940s as local, not-for-profit, mutual health insurers provide today, under the name The Associated Group, scores of health and financial services products to nearly three million people across the nation.

Though the company has evolved greatly both in scope and diversity from its founding to the present—total assets stand at $1.5 billion—it has not changed in its commitment to service, to customers, and to responsibility to the community. That corporate commitment has held firm from its founding in 1944 to today—through more than four decades of change and growth in the world, the nation, the state, and the city—as a sampling of key events in its history will attest.

Yesterday: A sense of tradition

Founding, 1944: Blue Cross of Indiana was founded to provide hospital insurance the same year the Allies invaded Normandy and turned the tide of war in Europe.

Founding, 1946: Blue Shield of Indiana, the medical counterpart to Blue Cross of Indiana, was founded and began writing business.That same year in New York City, the newly formed United Nations held its first session.

Growth, 1950s: The 1950s saw rapid growth in both Blue Cross and Blue Shield business as the nation enjoyed a postwar boom. The dec-ade also saw the world's first transistor radio (made in Indianapolis).

Expansion, 1966: Blue Cross and Blue Shield of Indiana began administering the Medicare program in Indiana under a contract with the federal government that greatly increased the number of people served. That same year, far above the Earth, Surveyor 1 sent back pictures from the surface of the moon.

Expansion, 1970: Having proven their skill with Medicare, Blue Cross and Blue Shield of Indiana also obtained a contract with the state to administer the Medicaid program, further adding to the number of people served. That same year Unigov went into operation and I-465 opened.

Restructuring, 1972: Otis "Doc" Bowen was elected governor of Indiana the same year Blue Cross and Blue Shield of Indiana signed a joint operating agreement to improve service and increase productivity—the first of several restructuring steps to position the companies for the future. That year President Nixon and Soviet leader Brezhnev signed the planet's first nuclear arms treaty.

Segmentation, 1982: Blue Cross and Blue Shield of Indiana began the process of segmentation to better position itself to serve individual markets. In the Hoosier capital, Indianapolis thrust itself into the national limelight by hosting the National Sports Festival, with 2,500 athletes competing before a quarter of a million spectators.

Merger, 1985: Blue Shield of Indiana was merged into Blue Cross of Indiana in the next step of stream-lining and reorganizing the company to compete in tomorrow's market. The company's new name: Associated Insurance Companies, Inc., now doing business as The Associated Group. In Indianapolis a downtown building boom began.

Diversification and expansion, 1986: Americans from coast to coast celebrated the hundredth anniversary of the Statue of Liberty the same year The Associated Group began a diversification and expansion strategy to reach new markets with highly specialized products. That same year Indianapolis was gearing up to host athletes and spectators from around the world at the Pan Am Games.

Acordia, 1988: The Associated Group began forming downstream distribution and administration companies focused on specific markets. These companies took the name Acordia and began marketing in Indiana and beyond.

The present: Today, as changes sweep the globe, as the state and nation face a new decade, and as Indianapolis continues its economic and cultural growth, The Associated Group moves into a bright future.

Tomorrow: A sense of vision.

As it moves ahead, The Associated Group is confident of that future. This company has seen nearly a half century of growth and change—within itself as well as in the community, the state, the nation, and the world. These changes forge a strong market economy to provide new and better products to ever wider markets.

The Associated Group is privileged to have served the people of Indianapolis and Indiana these many years, and looks forward to a future of even greater opportunity to serve customers and community.

Baker & Daniels

For more than 125 years, Baker & Daniels has been meeting the legal needs of Indiana clients. The firm was founded in 1863 by Thomas A. Hendricks, one of Indiana's most prominent citizens. Hendricks' career included service as a member of the U.S. House of Representatives, a U.S. Senator, Governor of Indiana, and Vice President of the United States.

Hendricks first practiced law in Shelbyville, then moved to Indianapolis and made an unsuccessful bid for governor as the Democratic candidate in 1860. Three years later, he was elected to the United States Senate and invited Indiana Attorney General Oscar B. Hord to join him in the practice of law, creating what is now the firm of Baker & Daniels.

In 1868, Hendricks again ran for governor, this time against the incumbent Republican Conrad Baker. Baker won by 961 votes. In 1872, Hendricks sought the governorship for a third time and was elected. Conrad Baker, the retiring governor and Hendricks' former foe, then joined the firm. When Hendricks' gubernatorial term expired, he returned to the firm in 1876.

Prior to 1880, two young lawyers were added to the firm: Albert Baker, son of Conrad and a graduate of Wabash College, and Edward Daniels, a fellow Wabash graduate. In 1889, the firm was renamed Baker & Daniels.

Some of the firm's earliest clients include the Indianapolis Water Company, Eli Lilly and Company, Foster and Bennett Lumber Company, The Great Lakes Trust Company, and The Snow Steam Pump Works.

What began as primarily a general practice law firm is today a firm of over 200 professionals providing a full range of services to diverse groups from international corporations to small local businesses and individuals. The firm has offices in Indianapolis, Fort Wayne, South Bend, and Washington, D.C.

After nearly seventy-five years in the old Fletcher Trust Building, in May of 1989, the firm relocated to a new facility. Baker & Daniels now occupies the twentieth through the twenty-seventh floors of 300 North Meridian Street.

In the fall of 1989, Baker & Daniels became the first Indiana law firm to acquire a nonlegal subsidiary corporation, Sagamore Associates. Sagamore is a Washington, D.C. based legislative consulting group that has enhanced the firm's presence in the Capital and provides its clients well-rounded representation with diverse capabilities.

Baker & Daniels is proud of being an involved member of the Indianapolis Chamber of Commerce. Firm members have served in a variety of capacities with the Chamber throughout its history, and the firm of Baker & Daniels looks forward to continuing this relationship.

Baker & Daniels moved to this 300 N. Meridian building in May 1989 and became its primary tenant, occupying the top seven floors.

BANK ONE, INDIANAPOLIS, NA

The roots of BANK ONE, INDIAN-APOLIS, NA (formerly American Fletcher National Bank and Trust Company) go deep in the history of Indianapolis, spanning 150 years. In its formative years the bank had many name changes. Its family tree comprises more than thirty-four bank mergers or acquisitions.

It all started in 1839 when a young man named Stoughton A. Fletcher came to Indianapolis with $3,000 in capital and started a bank which became known as the S. A. Fletcher Company. By 1872, the privately owned bank had acquired deposits of $643,541, and in 1898, it changed its original charter to become Fletcher National Bank. In 1910, Fletcher National Bank and American National Bank were merged to become Fletcher American National Bank. Fletcher American merged with National City Bank in 1924.

Three major lines contributed substantially to the present bank's stature: the A. Metzger Agency, a private bank established in 1863; the American National Bank, organized in 1901; and the Fidelity Trust Company, founded in 1909.

The A. Metzger Agency was established during the Civil War by persons of largely Germanic background. In 1906, it was rechartered as the German American Trust Company.

A friendly competitor of the bank was the Marion Trust Company, organized in 1895. In 1912, the two joined forces, resulting in the Fletcher Savings and Trust Company. Fletcher Savings began a period of rapid growth after World War I, merging through the 1920s with a number of smaller Indianapolis banks which became branches. In 1931, the name was shortened to Fletcher Trust Company, primarily a savings bank and trust company and a leader in the field of private and corporate trust administration. In 1954, the Fletcher Trust Company and the American National Bank of Indianapolis consolidated as the American Fletcher National Bank and Trust Company.

The third line of descent is attributable to a one-man powerhouse, Frank E. McKinney, Sr., banker, national politician, sportsman and civic leader. Dedicated to Indianapolis' growth, McKinney purchased Fidelity Trust Company in 1935. During the next two decades, under his guidance, a complex series of mergers and acquisitions took place. Fidelity merged with Bankers Trust Company in 1956, resulting in Fidelity Bank & Trust Company, which in 1959 merged with American Fletcher National Bank and Trust Company.

Under the Bank Holding Company Act of 1956, on December 31, 1968, American Fletcher National Bank became one of three banks in the country to be part of a one-bank holding company structure, with its parent company being named American Fletcher Corporation. During the next two decades, under the leadership of Frank E. McKinney, Jr., the bank grew to become the largest bank in the state in 1972, and it grew to approximately $4 billion in assets at year-end 1986.

On January 26, 1987, American Fletcher Corporation was acquired by BANC ONE CORPORATION, a multibank holding company from Columbus, Ohio, and the name of the bank was changed to BANK ONE, INDIANAPOLIS, NA.

Completed in December, 1989, the forty-eight story BANK ONE CENTER/TOWER, the third building in the complex, stands as the tallest building in the state of Indiana. BANK ONE, INDIANAPOLIS, NA occupies floors 4-19 and the 48th floor.

BANC ONE CORPORATION operates 52 banking organizations and 716 branch offices in Indiana, Kentucky, Michigan, Ohio, Wisconsin, and Texas. BANC ONE CORPORATION also operates several additional affiliates that engage in trust services, mortgage banking, consumer finance, equipment leasing, credit-related life insurance, investment management, data processing, discount brokerage, and venture capital activities.

Shown in this 1965 photograph are two of the three buildings that make up the BANK ONE CENTER complex, BANK ONE CENTER/CIRCLE and BANK ONE CENTER/FLETCHER.

140

Barnes & Thornburg

The Indianapolis Star, October 9, 1940

Early in the summer of 1940, four relatively young Indianapolis lawyers began to meet almost nightly in a particular room of the Indianapolis Athletic Club. Throughout the summer they had long discussions about the essential qualities of an ideal law firm. They had been brought together by a shared feeling that the three firms of which they were then a part, while well respected and successful, were not completely satisfactory. They had a common ambition to create a new firm which might more nearly approach their concepts of the ideal firm.

They finally agreed to form a new law firm. They pledged to each other that their new firm would be dedicated to professional excellence and to public service. To reach those fundamental goals, new additions to the firm would be recruited from the brightest and most ambitious law school graduates from the best law schools. After coming into the firm, those bright young associates would be rigorously trained by more experienced lawyers. Because the day of practicing law as a generalist was past, every lawyer would have to be skilled and experienced in a particular field of the law. Finally, each individual lawyer would have to be active in civic and community affairs of his choice. The name of the new law firm would be Barnes, Hickam, Pantzer and Boyd. (The four are pictured above.)

The long discussions ended with enthusiastic handshakes of agreement on Friday, September 13. In addition to that ominous fact, they observed that the thirteen rooms of their new law office on the thirteenth floor of the Merchants Bank Building would be occupied by thirteen people. Deciding that this omen should be considered good rather than evil, they quickly agreed that their new address and telephone number would also be 1313 and the license plates of every lawyer would be 1313. Triskaidekaphilia had set in.

The omen of 13 has proven a good one. The firm has prospered and grown far beyond the dream of those four original partners. That law firm is now Barnes & Thornburg, the largest in the state of Indiana, with over 200 lawyers rendering every type of legal

service throughout the country from its five offices located in Indianapolis, South Bend, Elkhart, Fort Wayne, and Washington, D.C. While there have been vast changes in the world and in the practice of law since those handshakes were exchanged in 1940, the fundamental principles agreed upon by those founding fathers remain paramount. The firm still competes with the best law firms here and throughout the country to secure the best and brightest students from the best law schools. It still offers its associates the same rigorous training. And even though the practice of law has become ever more time consuming and demanding, the firm is pleased that a Barnes & Thornburg lawyer is usually found among those engaged in worthwhile civic endeavors.

The firm's home is still the Merchants Bank Building, but instead of occupying a small space on the thirteenth floor, it now occupies eight and one-half floors, and expansion continues. Through the years, the firm became so sentimentally attached to this grand old building with its high ceilings and paneled walls that it became the building's owner in 1981. The firm has confidence that the building will continue to serve it well and be its home for many years to come.

The Merchants Bank Building, home to Barnes & Thornburg since 1940.

Business Furniture Corporation

Business Furniture Corporation (second building on left) at 122 E. Maryland Street in 1925.

Business Furniture Corporation was established in 1922 by C. S. Ober. The company began business at 42 S. Pennsylvania Street before moving in 1924 to 112 E. Maryland Street, where it operated for thirty-two years.

The company grew rapidly by concentrating on meeting the office furniture needs of Indianapolis businesses. As offices became more sophisticated, so did the services of Business Furniture Corporation. Warehousing, installation, and project management were among the services added to meet changing customer needs. The company quickly became, and remains today, the largest office furniture dealership in the state of Indiana.

In 1954 C. S. Ober became chairman of the board, and his son, John Ober, became president and chief executive officer. In need of new facilities to meet their rapidly growing business, the Obers purchased the structure across the street at 101 S. Pennsylvania Street

and moved the entire operation there in 1956.

Business Furniture Corporation was purchased by Debra and Richard Oakes in 1987. Both had been in management positions with Steelcase Inc. before deciding to purchase an office furniture dealership. Business Furniture Corporation was selected for its dominant market position in Indianapolis and its potential for increased growth through the nineties.

In developing the company since its purchase, the new owners have focused on increasing customer satisfaction, believing that to be the key to future growth in the office furniture industry. Customer feedback about all aspects of the company is gathered regularly for Business Furniture Corporation managers' use toward making improvements at all levels in the company. The combined efforts of all eighty employees resulted in corporate sales revenue of $21.5 million in 1989.

Placed on the National Register of Historic Places, the headquarters for Business Furniture Corporation has undergone extensive renovation and reflects the trend toward "adaptive re-use" of old buildings in the downtown area.

Citizens Gas & Coke Utility is a municipal public charitable trust, unique in this nation. It operates a distribution utility supplying gas service to slightly fewer than a quarter of a million customers in Indiana's state capital. It has no stockholders, pays no dividends, is not subject to political patronage, and is free from federal taxation. Its sole purpose is to supply safe, reliable, and effective gas service to the residents of the city of Indianapolis and Marion County, *at cost.*

The Utility traces its history to the first gas trust in Indianapolis, the Consumers Gas Trust Company, which was established in 1887, on the eve of this state's great, but all too short, natural gas boom around the turn of the last century. That predecessor trust was organized by

Eventually, as planned, ownership of the Citizens Gas Company was transferred to the city of Indianapolis in 1935, to be held in trust by the city for its residents.

Since 1935 the trust has been carried on under its trade name of the Citizens Gas & Coke Utility. The more full and formal designation of the Utility is:

City of Indianapolis by and through its Board of Directors for Utilities of its Department of Public Utilities, a municipal corporation of the State of Indiana, as successor

A view of Battery No. 1, 5-meter coke ovens operated by the Manufacturing Division of Citizens Gas & Coke Utility. The ovens are located at the Prospect Street Plant, 2950 Prospect Street. They produce two basic products: coke oven gas, which is mixed with natural gas as part of the gas supply for customers of the utility, and foundry and blast furnace coke, which is marketed nationally as Indianapolis Coke. Shown are the coal bunker (top), in which pulverized and blended coals are stored before being transported to the ovens for a baking process which produces a variety of cokes, and along the lower portion of the photo, the oven doors.

Opened November 1989, the Customer Service Center of Citizens Gas & Coke Utility is housed in a two-story addition to the utility's General Office building at 2020 N. Meridian Street.

a group of public spirited people (including Col. Eli Lilly, the founder of the international drug firm that bears his name) as an innovative amalgam of business efficiency, public benefit, and accountability.

With the depletion of natural gas in Indiana, the originators of the first gas trust company were forced to recreate the trust in 1906 as the Citizens Gas Company. In both companies, control was delivered to trustees to hold in perpetuity.

trustee of a public charitable trust, d/b/a Citizens Gas & Coke Utility.

The Utility is operated pursuant to a unique Indiana statute, Indiana Code 8-1-11.1, which applies only to it. Since the Utility is a municipal corporation, it pays no federal taxes, although it does pay all state and local taxes.

Today, the Utility supplies a mixture of natural gas and artificial gas manufactured as a by-product of its

coking operations at some of the lowest gas rates of any similarly situated U.S. snow-belt city. Selling under the brand name "Indianapolis Coke," it maintains a position as a major merchant coke manufacturer in both the foundry and blast furnace coke markets. Since 1969, the Utility has been a producer of crude oil discovered when exploring for and developing its extensive underground gas storage fields and facilities in Greene County, Indiana. All profits made in coke manufacturing and oil production are reinvested in its business or used directly to reduce the cost of gas service to its customers.

Community Hospitals Indianapolis

Two members of Community Hospital's first board of directors, Robert Efroymson, president, and John R. Dunigan, secretary, stand on the east side of the hospital's building site in the 1950s.

Community Hospitals Indianapolis is the city's largest health care system. With three hospitals, six MedCheck immediate medical care centers, and a variety of specialized services, Community serves thousands of area citizens every year.

Fewer than forty years ago, it was just a patch of land on which the residents of a growing east side placed their dreams for better, more accessible health care.

After World War II, Indianapolis grew toward the suburbs. Hospitals were crowded, and most were far from the citizens of the city's east side. To champion the cause of quality, accessible health care for the entire city, Edward Gallahue led a concerned civic group to form the Indianapolis Hospitals Development Association. Part of their challenge was to build a new east side hospital on land donated by Gallahue for that purpose at 16th Street and Ritter Avenue.

As the first board of directors for the hospital was assembled, funds poured in from the entire community: business, industry, and private citizens. Volunteers conducted house-to-house campaigns.

Employees in several companies donated funds through payroll deduction. *The East Side Herald* dubbed it "the swiftest, most effective fund raising campaign of our time." Today, the hospital still serves patients who proudly say, "I helped build this hospital."

Hundreds of Indianapolis citizens and then Vice President Richard M. Nixon attended the groundbreaking for the newly named Community Hospital. Then on August 6, 1956, with a full staff in place, Community Hospital opened its doors and admitted its first patient.

Since then, the hospital has expanded six times, has been renamed Community Hospital East, and has developed into part of a city-wide health care system: Community Hospitals Indianapolis. In 1985, as the city's northeast side grew rapidly, the system built Community Hospital North, a full-service hospital at 82nd and Shadeland to serve that area's expanding population. Also in the 1980s, Community opened what now number six MedChecks for neighborhood residents' immediate medical care needs.

In 1989, the city's south side had become another area of rapid growth and development, and Community again expanded into a growing population. On September 25, Community acquired University Heights Hospital, now Community Hospital South, with a commitment to expand services. This newest hospital sits at 1402 East County Line Road South, near Greenwood Park Mall.

As Community Hospitals Indianapolis continues to grow, it offers solid acute medical and surgical services at each hospital and a variety of specialized health care programs. Services include a full range of cardiovascular services; mental health services for all ages, both inpatient and outpatient; the Indiana Regional Cancer Center; the Hook Rehabilitation Center; older adults services; Neurocare Services; and women's and children's services, including maternity care and pediatrics. Other services include outpatient surgery; Family Home Health Care; emergency services; laser surgery; The Opti-Fast Program; and several other programs and services.

Community citizens founded this hospital to serve their health care needs. As Community Hospitals Indianapolis continues to grow, it keeps that important history always in mind.

Then-Vice President Richard M. Nixon joins others at the formal groundbreaking ceremony starting Community Hospital's construction.

In 1910, three Indiana lawyers founded Henley Matson & Gates. The direct-line successor of that firm is today composed of 145 lawyers. It is now known as Ice Miller Donadio & Ryan.

Ice Miller Donadio & Ryan

Ice Miller Donadio & Ryan, 1960: first row, far left, James V. Donadio; to his left, Harry T. Ice; far right, George P. Ryan; to his right, Merle H. Miller

During the 1980s, as the world has continued to become smaller and the economy of the world has become more integrated, the scope of the firm's practice has also increasingly included international transactions.

As an Indianapolis-based enterprise, the firm thinks of itself and its lawyers as citizens of Indiana and of Indianapolis, with all of the responsibilities and obligations that citizenship properly entails. Its lawyers are therefore heavily involved as volunteers in a wide range of citizens' activities, including arts organizations, social agencies, political affairs, and associations concerned with the legal profession.

Firmly committed to Indianapolis and Indiana, Ice Miller Donadio & Ryan looks forward to its role during the next 100 years of the Indianapolis Chamber of Commerce.

Historically as well as currently, American society is uniquely legalistic. Since the colonial period, the American impulse has been to cry, "There ought to be a law . . . !" The result is that the U.S. legal system is dynamic. It is affected by a number of factors, including the economy and political events, worldwide, national and local. Changes in American attitudes toward rights, both human and property, and the appropriate role of government in the affairs of the people also have a profound effect upon the nature of the law. Either abruptly or slowly, such factors work their way into legislative enactments, court decisions, and the rules and regulations of local, state, and federal bureaucracies.

Ice Miller Donadio & Ryan has always believed that the obligation of a law firm is to be sensitive to these changes, to anticipate them when possible, and promptly to

position the firm so that it is authoritatively prepared to advise clients when the clients are confronted by changes in the law.

Because of the complexity and dynamic character of the law, the firm in 1940 relied on the model of the medical profession and decided that it was not feasible for each lawyer to master the field as a whole. The general practitioner was perceived as obsolete. Accordingly, the firm adopted the specialization principle. Since 1940, each of its lawyers has concentrated on a particular specialized field and has sought and maintained expertise in that field. The consequence is that the firm as a whole is identified as a "full service" firm with the capacity to represent its clients in the always-expanding range of fields of the law. This is accomplished by having available specialists in each of the fields.

Samuel R. ''Chic'' Born (President, Indianapolis Bar Association, 1988-89), Leland B. Cross, Jr. (seated, Chairman, Indiana Chamber of Commerce, 1989-90), and John A. Grayson (President, Indiana State Bar Association, 1989-90)

INB National Bank

INB National Bank has a history closely allied with the history of banking in Indiana.

INB's roots date back to 1834, when the General Assembly granted a charter to the State Bank of Indiana, the state's first bank. The State Bank of Indiana, headquartered in Indianapolis, had branches throughout the state. The first board meeting of the Indianapolis branch was held on November 11, 1834, and marked the birth of the family of banks that were predecessors of INB.

In 1851, public opinion frowned on the state-owned bank monopoly, so during the 1851 state Constitutional Convention, the Constitution was written to encourage privately owned, independent banks.

Recognizing that the State Bank's charter was due to expire in 1859, the directors undertook action that ultimately resulted in the charter of a private bank. The bill to charter the new bank passed in 1854, and the Bank of the State of Indiana was born in 1857.

In the following decade, the Bank of the State of Indiana turned in its charter for a national charter under a new name: The Indiana National Bank of Indianapolis. The new bank set up shop at 15 North Meridian Street, the site of the present King Cole Building.

Several changes occurred in the 1890s. The Indiana General Assembly authorized the organization of loan, trust, and safe deposit companies in 1893. In 1895, a fire destroyed the Washington Street bank building, and a new building was begun at 3 Virginia Avenue. That building was completed in 1897 and occupied the same site that was the home of the Indianapolis branch of the State Bank of Indiana between 1840 and 1856.

This location served as home for The Indiana National Bank for seventy-three years.

As the nineteenth century ended, Indiana National was still basically a commercial bank. Only businesses and wealthy individuals had checking accounts.

The decade of the 1920s was one of new beginnings. The bank was processing 5,000 checks daily and began sending monthly checking statements to customers in the early 1920s. In 1921, the bank opened a savings department. The first day's receipts totaled $1,754. Five years later, savings accounts totaled $1 million.

Indiana National survived the devastating era of bank failures following the stock market crash of 1929. It was one of the few large banks that the government did not have to help with preferred stock during this difficult time.

Indiana National continued its tradition of expansion. Although World War II delayed some expansion plans, the end of the war found Indiana National first among Indiana banks. The bank's first branch, on "suburban" 38th Street, was opened in 1947. Indiana

National's first computer was installed at 41 East Washington Street in 1962, and three years later an enlarged computer center and new mortgage loan headquarters opened.

A milestone was reached in 1962. The June 30 statement showed resources of the bank at over $1 billion, the first time any Indiana bank topped the billion-dollar mark. In 1967, construction of the Indiana National Bank Tower was underway. Destined to remain the tallest building in Indiana for more than a decade, the Tower's construction reaffirmed the bank's commitment to the central city and is credited with initiating the renaissance of downtown Indianapolis.

In 1969, a one-bank holding company was formed and named Indiana National Corporation. The bank changed its name from The Indiana National Bank of Indianapolis to The Indiana National Bank and has since remained the principal subsidiary of the corporation. Indiana Mortgage Corporation became the first non-bank subsidiary.

A new identity, acquisition activity and a new name dominated the 1980s. Indiana National entered the decade with a new identity featuring a Bison symbol. The new look reflects the bank's tie to the state's history while emphasizing those qualities it hopes to impart to its publics: strength, trust, tradition and steadfastness.

After a number of bank acquisitions in the mid through late 1980s, the corporation, along with all of its subsidiaries, streamlined its name to INB. The original bank founded in 1834 is now known as INB National Bank.

INB's tradition is worthy of pride and inspires the company's continued concentration in banking and bank-related pursuits. INB's history has proven that banking and financial services are what it does best and will continue to be INB's focus in the future.

The Indianapolis News

The Indianapolis News at its 30 West Washington Street location.

A dynamic, independent, low-cost newspaper that published the news the same day it happened was the dream of John H. Holliday, the newspaperman who brought *The Indianapolis News* to life 121 years ago.

At the time, 1869, John Holliday was a reporter for *The Indianapolis Sentinel.* In what must have been a masterful demonstration of salesmanship, he persuaded his management to allow him to use the *Sentinel*'s equipment to produce a competing newspaper. Holliday believed his dream would succeed because of three innovations:

1. Timeliness. A faster system for organizing the publishing cycle would enable him to print the news the same day it happened.

2. Independent editorial policy. In those days, newspapers were extremely partisan to attract both readers and advertisers. Holliday, however, planned to be independent, "being the organ of neither individual, sect or party."

3. Low cost. The evening *News* would sell for two cents, a penny less than the city's other newspapers. It was the first two-cent newspaper published west of Pittsburgh.

Holliday proved his point about timeliness when his first issue, published December 6, 1869, carried the text of an address made that day to the Congress by President U.S. Grant.

By the time ill health forced Holliday to sell *The News* in 1892, it had become the most influential newspaper in the state. The buyer of record was William H. Smith of Chicago, but the majority ownership of the paper was held by Charles Warren Fairbanks.

In 1948, Eugene C. Pulliam purchased controlling interest in *The News* from the Fairbanks family. Pulliam, who began his newspaper career in Kansas, was the owner of several other newspapers, including *The Indianapolis Star.* He immediately began consolidating and streamlining the production and business operations of the two newspapers. By moving *The News* into quarters adjacent to those of *The Star* at 307 N. Pennsylvania Street, he was able to combine the mechanical operations and pass the savings on to the readers in the form of increased news coverage and many more features. Today, the business functions, circulation, and advertising sales for both newspapers are also handled together. However, the newspapers themselves continue to have completely separate editorial operations, competing avidly to provide good news coverage.

Eugene C. Pulliam died in June 1975 at age 86. Eugene S. Pulliam succeeded his father as publisher of both *The News* and *The Star.* The daily publication of *The News* is the responsibility of Managing Editor Frank Caperton (news gathering operation) and Editor Harvey Jacobs (editorial and op-ed pages). Together they work to insure that *The Indianapolis News* continues to serve its community.

The Indianapolis News, the oldest newspaper in Indianapolis, was the first successful evening paper in the city. Today, it is the largest evening newspaper in Indiana, publishing about 115,000 copies each weekday. Over 100 persons are involved in its writing, editing, and photography.

Indianapolis Newspapers, Inc. has installed and is operating four high speed, "state of the art" offset presses capable of producing crisp, bright half tones or pictures and multi-colored pages at speeds of more than 1,000 papers per minute.

Additionally, one more offset press is being installed and should be in operation by late 1990. When this modernization program is completed, *The Indianapolis News* and *The Indianapolis Star* will be printed on presses equal or superior to those at any newspaper in the world.

Indianapolis Power & Light Company

Employees such as these two members of the Indianapolis Power & Light Company's Street Lighting Department were responsible for cleaning the globes that covered the city's street lights in the 1920s.

Electric service in Indianapolis began January 11, 1882, when arc lights were lit in the former Union Railway Station on South Illinois Street. Pioneering this innovative energy form was Indianapolis Brush Electric Light & Power Company, one of eleven predecessors of Indianapolis Power & Light Company (IPL).

Those early lights were inefficient, dim, and expensive to operate. They were far superior to the commonly used gas lamps. *The Indiana Journal* reported, "The display was very satisfactory and was admired by many people. The depot was lighter than it has been since the roof was put on. . . ."

Initially, electric service was available only from 1 P.M. to 1 A.M. in the immediate downtown, and only for commercial lighting. Despite limitations, 165 applications were received for the new electricity during the first week, however, customers soon received continuous service. This marked the start

of IPL's long tradition of striving to improve customer service.

Electricity demand grew along with Indianapolis, and by the 1920s had moved from a curiosity to a necessity. Numerous appliances for the home, and larger and more efficient motors to power industry, made life more enjoyable and more productive. Record investments in new facilities were made, but it became apparent that duplicate sets of poles, wires, and generating plants were costly for customers.

On October 27, 1926, Indianapolis Light & Heat Company and Merchants Heat & Light Company merged to form the present Indianapolis Power & Light Company. The new company's first acts were to reduce electric rates, eliminate some 125 miles of duplicate lines, and begin construction of a new generating station.

An interesting sidelight concerns Merchants Heat & Light employees

who devoted many off-hours to modifying one of the company's surplus radio transmitters to accommodate regular radio broadcasting. They received a license, and WFBM Radio debuted on November 4, 1924. The station was operated by Indianapolis Power & Light Company as a community public service until its sale in 1939.

In 1940, because of the Public Utility Holding Act of 1935, all of the common stock of IPL was sold to some 8,000 shareholders. Indianapolis Power & Light Company became the first major electric utility, as a subsidiary of a holding company, to be publicly owned.

This partnership of confidence and trust between the company and the public has continued through the years, as IPL has provided the community even greater amounts of reliable electric power at reasonable cost. The company is proud that it has always met customer demand with no reduction in service. And electric rates for Indianapolis remain among the lowest of the twenty largest U.S. cities served by investor-owned utilities. IPL is committed to continuing this tradition of unsurpassed service to its customers.

This four-story building at 48 Monument Circle, built in 1897 as the office of the old Indianapolis Light and Power Company, also was the first general office of the modern IPL.

Jenn-Air Company

Jenn-Air Company continues to be an appliance industry innovator with products such as the Dual-Fuel™ grill-range, the world's first range with a down-draft-ventilated gas grill-range cooktop and an electric oven.

New first-in-the-industry kitchen appliances streaming out of the Jenn-Air plant at 3035 Shadeland are evidence that the company's tradition of developing innovative products continues.

The Dual-Fuel™ grill-range and the electric outdoor grills of the 1990s take their place on a list that includes the introduction in 1967 of the first downdraft-ventilated grill-ranges and cooktops that make indoor grilling possible. With these products, Jenn-Air set the standard for luxury in cooking appliances, a standard still being emulated by the industry—and continued by Jenn-Air.

The Dual-Fuel grill-range introduced in late 1989 is the first range in the world that combines a down-draft-ventilated gas grill-range cooktop and a self-cleaning electric oven. In 1990 came another industry first: the first electric grill UL-approved for outdoor installation.

In fact, the company's history can be recorded in its list of firsts. It entered the home appliance field in 1961 with the residential appliance industry's first range and oven with built-in ventilation. Next came, in 1965, the first downdraft-

ventilated range, and two years later, the grill-range. In 1972, Jenn-Air introduced the first convertible grill-range cooktop with plug-in cooktop cartridges that give cooks the ability to design their own ranges. The Jenn-Air Selective-Use™ oven, which can be used as either a convection oven or as a radiant (conventional) oven, made its entry in 1975 as a "first." In 1983, the company achieved another first when it met the challenge of engineering an induction cooktop cartridge.

The breadth of Jenn-Air's product line has also grown. It is now possible to have an all-Jenn-Air kitchen, including dishwasher, refrigerator, microwave oven, trash compactor, and disposer, as well as cooking appliances. The choice in cooking appliances has broadened to include gas as well as electricity, and updraft ventilated ranges and cooktops, both with and without grills. Jenn-Air range hoods are available also.

Since 1982 Jenn-Air has been a division of Maytag Corporation—and has seen sales grow by 167 percent in that time. The company was founded in 1947 by inventor Louis J. Jenn, who sold it in 1979 to Car-

rier Corporation. First products were commercial and industrial ventilation systems. (This operation became a separate business unit, Jenn Industries, in 1975 and was purchased by Maytag along with Jenn-Air Company; Maytag sold Jenn Industries in 1989.)

Currently, Jenn-Air has 882,000 square feet of manufacturing, warehouse, and office space on Shadeland Avenue and employs 850 people. The factory was built in 1965 and first expanded two years later.

A $26.5-million headquarters office and factory expansion program was initiated in 1985 to create a state-of-the-art facility for the production of upscale, quality appliances. Electric grill-ranges and cooktops, gas grill-range cooktops, the Dual-Fuel grill-range, and wall ovens are produced there.

As part of the latest expansion and update program, Jenn-Air acquired adjacent property for future requirements. As Jenn-Air approaches the twenty-first century, with Donald M. Lorton as president, the company is positioned to grow both in product development and facility expansion.

New headquarter offices were one part of Jenn-Air's recent expansion project at its facility at 3035 N. Shadeland.

Lacy Diversified Industries, Ltd.

William Howard Taft was closing out his White House years when Howard J. Lacy, Sr., laid out $343 on April 12, 1912, as a down payment on a corrugator and formed the U.S. Corrugated-Fibre Box Company.

The company grew and prospered for nearly seven decades and, before its sale in 1984, became the foundation for a new and richly diversified company called Lacy Diversified Industries, a holding company created in 1972. This evolution, which now spans four generations of Lacys, has taken the company far beyond its Indiana roots, resulting in a national corporation with holdings in nineteen states.

The founding Lacy built the box company into a national power in its field, and by 1940 it was one of the largest in its industry. With his death in 1952, the management reins passed to Howard J. Lacy II, whose business career ended abruptly when he succumbed to a heart attack in 1959.

His widow, Edna Balz Lacy, who had been secretary and assistant treasurer of the firm since 1951, stepped into the breach as the new chairman. She became one of the first women CEOs in the city and with business acumen that surprised even her peers, took the company to unexpected heights in the 1960s.

A daughter, Margot, became a director in 1957, and a son, Andre, followed suit four years later. Edna Lacy, now 83, remains chairman of the company, and Andre has served as its president since 1978.

LDI began to diversify shortly after 1972 with the acquisition of Jessup Door Company, a manufacturer of top-of-the-line wood doors. The diversification strategy took on a new dimension in 1980 with adop-

tion of a strategic plan calling for acquisitions of selected distribution companies and the sale of its corrugated box company.

Currently, LDI, Ltd., is a limited partnership with net sales of approximately $300 million. Its holdings span the nation and employ more than a thousand people in nearly two dozen facilities. In addition to Jessup and its wood product subsidiaries, LDI owns Major Video Concepts, one of the country's largest distributors of prerecorded videocassettes, and Tucker-Rocky Inc., the country's largest distributor of accessories and after-market parts for the motorcycle industry.

Today, LDI is a multifaceted investment management company which maintains these wide-ranging business investments to maximize shareholder value—an objective achieved through its reputation for integrity, for quality employees, for superior products and service to customers, and for exemplary labor-management relations.

LDI also seeks to be a leader in demonstrating corporate social responsibility. Corporate personnel are actively involved in a host of civic endeavors, with special emphasis on the delivery of human services and on improving the quality of education and life in the communities where LDi is represented.

For almost half of the Indianapolis Chamber's history, at least one member of the Lacy family has figured prominently in the organization. Howard J. Lacy II was a long-time director and served two terms as its chairman in 1953 and 1954. Edna Lacy was elected a director in 1973, becoming the first woman ever named to the board, and was named a life director in

1987. Andre Lacy was chosen a Chamber director in 1989.

The Lacy family is best known in Chamber affairs for its sponsorship of an educational project that has paid huge dividends for the city. After a son died in a tragic auto accident in 1973, Edna Lacy established a foundation to commemorate him. Out of that effort evolved the Stanley K. Lacy Executive Leadership Series in 1976.

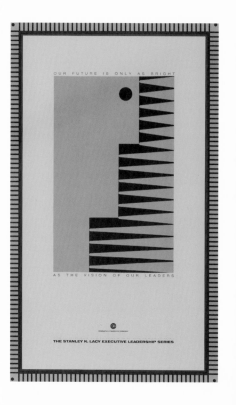

This program provides a nine-month training program for potential community leaders to learn more about community service opportunities and encourages them to participate in civic activities. So far over 350 men and women have participated in this educational experience, and the series has been widely copied across the nation as a means of engaging emerging leaders in community service.

Eli Lilly and Company

Josiah Kirby Lilly, Sr. (left), son of Col. Eli Lilly, and Ernest G. Eberhardt, the company's first full-time chemist, work in the firm's scientific laboratory in 1886.

On May 10, 1876, Col. Eli Lilly, a Civil War veteran, opened the doors of a small laboratory in downtown Indianapolis for the purpose of manufacturing high quality medications. An experienced pharmacist, Col. Lilly recognized the need for reliable prescription medicines at a time when patent medicines with unfounded curative claims dominated the drug field and duped the credulous.

The small business would become Eli Lilly and Company, a global research-based corporation that develops, manufactures, and markets pharmaceuticals, animal health products, medical instruments, and diagnostic products.

Deeply involved in the civic and business life of the city, Col. Lilly was a founding member of the Indianapolis Chamber of Commerce (then called the Commercial Club).

Eli Lilly and Company's first major scientific achievement involved the successful production of insulin. In 1921, the company learned of the discovery by Banting and Best at the University of Toronto that diabetes could be controlled by injections of an extract of pancreas. In a cooperative effort with the university, Lilly developed the production process and participated in the clinical trials. The initial development of insulin, derived from animal pancreases, was the foundation of modern diabetes management.

Lilly began to widen its research activity, which became central to the company's progress. For example, the Lilly Laboratory for Clinical Research was established in 1926 at Wishard Memorial Hospital (then City Hospital) in Indianapolis. Today, the clinic is one of the largest facilities of its kind in the pharmaceutical industry.

In 1939, the first manufacturing plant outside the United States began operations in Basingstoke, England. Rapid expansion occurred after World War II, with new plants, laboratories, and other facilities constructed and purchased in the U.S., Europe, Latin America, and elsewhere in the world.

Advances in Lilly agricultural research in the 1950s led to the company's entry into markets for animal health and plant science products. Major products have included animal health and nutrition products and agricultural chemicals.

The company's leadership in the field of antibiotic research led to the development and introduction in 1964 of the first of a new family of lifesaving antibiotics, the cephalosporins. Ceclor®, an oral cephalosporin introduced in 1979, had emerged as the world's number-one selling product in its class by 1987.

Diversification and acquisition characterized the late 1970s and the 1980s, as Lilly moved into new but related fields of medical instruments and diagnostic products. The subsidiaries, which make up the company's Medical Instrument Systems and Diagnostic Systems divisions, search for innovative products in the fields of technically advanced cardiovascular products, intravenous therapy, vital signs monitoring, and monoclonal-based diagnostics.

In recent years, research and development programs have targeted new areas of investigation that have resulted in the introduction of significant products. For example, Humulin®, human insulin, which was introduced in 1982, was the world's first human-health-care product based on recombinant DNA technology. Scientists used the new biotechnology to develop a process for making virtually unlimited quantities of insulin identical to the substance made by the human pancreas.

In 1988, Lilly introduced the antidepressant Prozac® to the U.S. market. A result of Lilly research, Prozac represents an important new class of antidepressant.

As Eli Lilly and Company looks to the future, it is focusing its resources on the application of high technology to the life sciences.

Ceclor® (cefaclor, Lilly)
Humulin® (human insulin of recombinant DNA origin, Lilly)
Prozac® (fluoxetine hydrochloride, Dista)

Cutting pills by hand in 1891 in the pill production area of Eli Lilly and Company.

Marsh Supermarkets

The original Marsh grocery store, circa 1931.

When Ermal Marsh came to Muncie in 1931 to attend Ball State Teacher's College, he opened a small grocery store to finance his education. His innovative marketing techniques quickly built his business, and by 1933 he had become successful enough to incorporate as Marsh Food Stores, Inc.

Marsh expanded his business, despite the Great Depression and food rationing during World War II, by unifying with other grocers to purchase goods in bulk. In 1947, the company opened its first major supermarket, the Marsh Foodliner, a large, self-service operation which generated profits three times greater than the original projection.

The company went public in 1949, with 40,000 shares of common stock to finance Ermal Marsh's newest idea, the Marsh Food Center in Yorktown. Officially opened in 1952, it served as a distribution warehouse and office facility.

Marsh became known for its marketing experiments, including food specialties. One such item, Marsh Ice Cream, became so successful that the Yorktown plant became the largest producer of gallon ice cream in the United States.

By its twenty-fifth anniversary, the company had attained annual sales of $34 million and a reputation as an industry leader. That year also marked the opening of the first Marsh store in Indianapolis.

The company lost its energetic leader when Ermal Marsh was killed in a 1959 plane crash. His brother, Estel, assumed the role of company president.

Marsh Supermarkets continued to provide its trademark, innovative customer service, and successfully developed the convenience store concept, opening ten Village Pantry units by 1968.

In 1968, Don E. Marsh replaced his uncle as president. The eldest son of Ermal Marsh had learned the business from the ground up, serving in many capacities from sacker to vice president.

Throughout the 1970s, Marsh remained an innovative leader in the industry. The world's first laser-scanning purchase was made at a Marsh store in 1974.

During the 1980s, Marsh used computer technology to improve customer service and expanded its community involvement as a sponsor of the Tenth Pan-American Games, Symphony on the Prairie, The Children's Museum, the Indianapolis Zoo and the Art Museum.

With annual sales approaching $1 billion, Marsh Supermarkets will enter the 1990s by moving its corporate offices to Indianapolis, where it does more than 40 percent of its business.

The Marsh family remains active in company operations, with Don Marsh as president and CEO, Alan Marsh, president of Village Pantry, and William L. Marsh, vice president/general manager of property management. The family's involvement ensures a continuation of the innovative business strategies that emphasize the company's philosophy and motto, "We Value You."

Always an industry leader, Marsh was the first supermarket in the world to use laser scanning of UPC codes and one of the first to offer debit and charge services to customers.

152

Merchants National Bank was founded in Indianapolis in January 1865, when five businessmen pledged a pool of $100,000 and declared themselves the first stockholders and directors of Merchants National Bank. It was the fourth national bank established in Indianapolis and is today the oldest national bank in the city.

In 1867, thirteen-year-old John Peter Frenzel was hired as a bank messenger. He was the first of what would become Indiana's oldest banking family.

During the next several years, two other Frenzel brothers, Otto and Oscar, would hold the job of bank messenger, as the family moved higher in the small organization.

Merchants grew with the city, as the bank provided support to many new businessmen, founders of some of today's largest businesses in the state. To serve the rapidly growing population, John and Otto Frenzel organized a travel and steamship agency under the name of Frenzel Brothers. They advertised "the most complete foreign office in the state."

In 1882, John and Otto Frenzel bought the stock holdings of retiring president Volney Mallott. At twenty-eight, John became the

Merchants National Bank and Trust Company

Merchants Plaza

youngest president of a national bank in the United States.

Merchants began construction of a seventeen-story downtown office building in 1908. When completed in 1913, it was the tallest building in the city and would remain so for the next fifty years.

In 1918, Merchants was the first to open Indianapolis neighborhood banks, forerunners of today's branch banking system. Together with its sister institution, the Indiana Trust Company, the bank stood strong through the Great Depression of the early 1930s.

During this time, another Frenzel was working his way up the ranks, beginning as a messenger after World War I. In the mid-1940s, Otto N. Frenzel, Jr. became president of the bank. He launched a business development program, brought in outside talent, and enlarged the bank's branch system. He also merged the Indiana Trust Company into the bank in 1953.

In 1970, Otto N. Frenzel, Jr. became chairman of the board, and his son, Otto N. Frenzel, III was named president. In 1971, the formation of a bank holding company called Merchants National Corporation was organized. Ground was broken for its headquarters, the $50 million Merchants Plaza building, in 1973.

The 1980s brought many changes at Merchants—among the most important was the expansion of Merchants National Corporation. The corporation is now the holding company for Merchants National Bank's forty-four branches, as well as for sixteen affiliates with more than ninety banking locations throughout Indiana.

Today, Otto N. Frenzel, III is chairman of the board of Merchants National Corporation, the second largest publicly held bank holding company in the state. James D. Massey is chairman of Merchants National Bank, and James W. Magee serves as president.

For over fifty years, Merchants Bank was the tallest building in Indianapolis. The building pictured is located at 11 S. Meridian St.

153

Park Fletcher, Inc.

Excerpt from a conversation with Floyd B. Kelsey, Chairman of the Board

My recollection of the origin of Park Fletcher goes back to the summer of 1961. The place was Fort Wayne, where in partnership with the Murchison family from Dallas, we were developing the first of the modern industrial parks in Indiana. Its name was Interstate Industrial Park.

Two gentlemen visited the construction site and introduced themselves as Fred Beyer, manager of industrial development for the Indianapolis Chamber of Commerce, and Roger Speidel, industrial development manager of the Pennsylvania Railroad.

After being briefed on our project, Beyer expressed an interest in our going to Indianapolis to develop a similar project. I introduced him to Sam W. Fletcher, president of Interstate Industrial Park, who then went to Indianapolis and was shown potential sites by a group headed by Beyer. On that trip, Fletcher selected the present site of Park Fletcher for a number of reasons, including its proximity to Weir Cook Airport, now Indianapolis International Airport, and its access to existing highways and proposed interstates including I-465 and I-70.

There was no question that the site was an excellent selection, but it did have the disadvantage of being comprised of more than fifty-five different parcels. R. J. Moore, then with W. A. Brennan Company, accepted the task of assembling the land and did so ahead of schedule.

Park Fletcher was incorporated in February 1962. Its list of directors and stockholders included top executives from two major banks, all the public utilities, a major newspaper, a top department store, and two prominent real estate firms, as well as Fletcher and a Murchison family representative. Two of the original incorporators, Fred Beyer and Carl Reis, continue to serve with me as directors.

Fletcher then selected the Frank Lloyd Wright Foundation to do initial planning of the park. By the summer of 1965, the first street construction was underway; at about the same time the Executive Drive bridge over Airport Expressway was being constructed by Park Fletcher. Sales, leases, and construction accelerated. A. B. Dick was the first company to move into the park. By the middle of 1965, management reported that nineteen companies had purchased or leased building sites in the 635-acre park. These included The Economy Company, Quality Gage, J. T. Pehler Wholesale, and Caterpillar Tractor. By the end of 1965, over 120 acres were being utilized by thirty-one firms, with 208,000 square feet of building.

In 1968, the company changed its thrust from the sale of building sites to building and leasing for its own account. Bruce Hartshorne became the local manager. A number of speculative single-occupancy buildings were built and were leased to Honeywell, Goodyear, and Reynolds Metals, among others. Multi-occupancy buildings soon followed and were widely accepted for their adaptability to space requirements.

Beginning in 1978, the financial strength of several insurance companies as partners was tapped to fuel faster growth. Today the company owns, manages, and leases approximately two million square feet in thirty-six buildings and accommodates activities in distribution, wholesale, research and development, and Class A office.

Park Fletcher Business Center is now home to over 300 companies, occupying 4.8 million square feet in 135 buildings and employing over 4,800 people. The future will include the development of the 120 acres of remaining building sites and a continued economic impact on Indianapolis.

Park Fletcher—Adjacent to Indianapolis International Airport with downtown Indianapolis in the background.

Railroadmen's Federal Savings and Loan Association

A highlight of Railroadmen's recent history was its conversion from a mutual savings and loan to a stockholder-owned Association in 1987. In 1988, it completed a merger with Heritage Federal Savings Bank in Elwood, thus expanding its market area into Madison County and allowing it to increase its stock offerings. Railroadmen's also expanded its operations in Marion County during 1988 with a new office in the growing College Park area of northwestern Indianapolis.

Today, Railroadmen's continues to operate as it always has—conservatively, with the best interests of its customers and shareholders foremost in mind. The company is proud of the progress it has made and is excited about new potentials for more. Railroadmen's line of services has been expanded, and the Association is eagerly seeking to expand its operations in central Indiana's most promising growth areas.

Much of the credit for the company's success goes to the city of Indianapolis and the surrounding counties. Railroadmen's does business in an excellent market area, which helps it attract the highest quality of customers and employees.

For its customers, Railroadmen's is committed to convenience and service-oriented banking. Furthermore, it intends to maintain a competitive position in the mortgage loan market. For its shareholders, the company will sustain and augment the marked financial success achieved in recent years. With loyal support and the dedication of its staff, Railroadmen's Federal Savings and Loan Association will continue to thrive and contribute positively to the Indianapolis business community of the future.

Carved out of swamp lands in 1821 to be the state's new capital, Indianapolis had its early detractors and skeptics. But it was the railroad that first linked the state of Indiana to other sectors of a growing regional economy. Indianapolis became one of the most important transportation hubs in the Midwest. The city's central location and excellent rail transportation network furthered its development as both a manufacturing and distribution center, with diverse opportunities for businesses and individuals alike.

By the late 1800s, Indianapolis was a boom town, replete with boom town temptations. In a single evening of merry-making, a railroad worker could easily go through a week's earnings. Realizing the need for thrift and savings, several railroadmen persuaded the paymaster to hold back a small portion of their wages each week. From this simple arrangement in 1887, Railroadmen's Federal Savings and Loan was born.

By founding the Association we know today as Railroadmen's, Indianapolis' early railroad workers made a major contribution to their city's growth. Through weekly contributions made at the Association's office in Indianapolis' Union Station, they helped build and buy homes for themselves and other members, bettering their families' living conditions as they supported the expansion of their city.

Through the years, Railroadmen's Federal Savings and Loan Association has maintained a commitment to the dream of home ownership that motivated those early railroad workers to saving. From the Victorian dwellings built by the railroadmen of 1887 to our city's newest cluster of condominiums, every neighborhood in Indianapolis contains homes financed by Railroadmen's.

Beginning in the early 1980s, the company implemented operating strategies designed to restructure its balance sheet and reduce exposure to interest rate risk. In addition, it has developed new products and markets to increase the competitiveness of its financial services while continuing to emphasize high asset quality.

155

Ransburg Corporation

Henry Ford revolutionized automobile manufacturing. George Eastman made photography accessible to millions of amateurs. What these two giants achieved in their respective industries, Indiana native Harold Ransburg accomplished in industrial finishing.

In the late 1930s, Ransburg invented the electrostatic painting process and irrevocably changed how products were coated. Today, the company he founded, the Indianapolis-based Ransburg Corporation, is a worldwide technology leader in the development of finishing systems.

As a young man, Harold Ransburg worked in his father's housewares business. Day after day, he watched the company waste literally hundreds of gallons of enamel spray painting its various flour canisters and cookie jars. Harold set out to find a more efficient method of coating products. The result was a painting technique based on electrostatic attraction: positively charging one article and negatively charging another, thereby creating a natural magnetic force between the two.

By the late 1940s, a number of well-known companies, such as A.C. Spark Plug and Dow Chemical, were using the Ransburg coating method. Rather than sell its product to manufacturing operations, Ransburg leased its coating equipment. The electrostatic painting process was protected by patents, and customers paid a license fee to Ransburg.

This lucrative structure, coupled with a truly innovative painting process which applied approximately 95 percent of the sprayed paint, generated steady profits for the modest Hoosier company. Established in 1948 as a separate corporate entity, the Ransburg

Testing the electrostatic painting process at Ransburg Corporation in the 1950s.

Today's automated electrostatic finishing system.

Corporation earned less than $100,000 in 1950. In 1962, however, the company made more than $1.3 million in net income. Five years later, the Ransburg Corporation went public.

In preparation for the 1976 expiration of its two most important U.S. patents, Ransburg in 1973 purchased Micro-Poise, a major supplier of mass production balancing machines headquartered in Indianapolis.

Beginning in the late seventies, the company embarked on an aggressive growth and acquisition program in an effort to diversify and strengthen its long-term economic future. This included an agreement with Renault Industries to form Cybotech, a joint venture industrial robot company. Also, Ransburg purchased three motor-winding businesses that manufactured

equipment to automate the production of electric motors.

Prospects looked bright until the country experienced a severe recession in the early 1980s which caused a drastic decrease in orders for capital equipment. In addition, the industrial robot market did not grow as rapidly as Ransburg expected and, in fact, started to decline. After the company had suffered losses, Cybotech and the motor-winding companies were sold.

In April 1989, Ransburg was acquired by ITW, a worldwide manufacturer of engineered components and industrial systems and consumables, with annual sales in excess of $2 billion.

Today, the Ransburg Corporation employs more than 1,000 at its operations in twelve countries, including major companies in the United States, Germany, Japan, Switzerland, and the Netherlands. Throughout the world, the company designs, produces, and sells electrostatic finishing systems to the major automobile and truck manufacturers, powder and liquid electrostatic finishing systems and equipment to industrial customers, and static control equipment to the electronic and industrial markets.

Since the company's inception, Ransburg has dedicated substantial financial resources to research. That trend continues today with Ransburg Global Technology, recently established in Japan to develop new finishing processes and products for worldwide automotive application. Ransburg has also formed two worldwide technology teams composed of employees from Ransburg's various international operations. Both groups meet on a regular basis to identify market needs and plan new technologies.

These investments in research and development, along with highly competent personnel, help insure Ransburg's economic future and continued contribution to the Indianapolis community.

St. Francis Hospital Center

The history of St. Francis Hospital Center can be traced to the late 1800s, half the world away in Olpe, Germany. There Mother Theresia Bonzel founded the Order of the Poor Sisters of St. Francis Seraph of the Perpetual Adoration.

Less than ten years later, Mother Theresia brought her fledgling community to Indiana, establishing a Provincial House in Lafayette in 1875. In 1906, Father Peter Killian, pastor of Holy Name Parish in Beech Grove, invited the Sisters to establish a hospital. Two representatives rode in an open buggy to accept Father Killian's invitation and to find a site for their new hospital.

That site, a five-acre tract at the intersection of Troy Avenue and Sherman Drive, became the home of St. Francis Hospital Center. The cornerstone was laid in 1913, and St. Francis opened its doors in 1914, featuring seventy-five beds and offering complete medical services.

The steady population increase in Beech Grove and Indianapolis placed a strain on the hospital by the 1920s. In 1931, to meet growing needs, St. Francis added its South Building, doubling the bed capacity. From 1945 through 1956, annual admissions at St. Francis tripled, and the hospital faced the insurmountable task of providing 1956 health care with 1931 facilities. This led to the opening of the 104-bed North Building.

Through the 1960s, with a focus on science and technology, St. Francis continued its leadership role by acquiring Indiana's first Betatron for cancer treatment, and the state's first Coulter blood analyzer. A computer center for all of the hospitals in the order was constructed at St. Francis during the 1960s, and in 1967, St. Francis established its School of Medical Technology.

As the 1970s began, groundbreaking ceremonies were held for the largest addition to the hospital, the Bonzel Towers. The Towers fea-

Two Sisters from the Provincial House in Lafayette, IN, traveled to Beech Grove in a horse-drawn buggy to select a site for St. Francis Hospital Center. They arranged for the purchase of five acres at a cost of $1,000.

tured private rooms, a fifteen-bed Cardiac Care Unit, a twelve-bed Intensive Care Unit, and a fully equipped Emergency Department. A Medical Arts Building and a parking garage were included in this construction project. The 1970s also saw St. Francis implement Computerized Tomography (CT) scanning in 1979.

The 1980s featured the addition of many outpatient services and the emergence of wellness and preventive healthcare. Services such as

Little did the Sisters realize that more than 75 years later St. Francis would be a sprawling, 540-bed institution providing care to hundreds-of-thousands of people each year.

occupational health, home health care, a minor emergency center, an off-campus counseling center, and several lifestyle improvement courses help St. Francis continue its role as a health care leader.

Other services added during the decade include geriatric services, cardiac catheterization and open heart surgery, and a comprehensive three-phase cardiac rehabilitation program. On the "firsts" front, in 1987 St. Francis conducted the Midwest's first aortic valvuloplasty. St. Francis' labor and delivery and ambulatory surgery areas also received significant facelifts during this decade.

St. Francis Hospital Center celebrated its seventy-fifth birthday in 1989, and the philosophy which guided the hospital through three quarters of a century continues to shape its growth for the future.

"As a healing institution serving nearly a quarter of a million patients each year, St. Francis Hospital Center mustn't rest on its successes of the past," said President and CEO Paul J. Stitzel. "Rather, we look at the present to determine how we can best serve the community. And we look to the future, to anticipate how health care needs will change, and how technology will allow us to administer the Sisters' healing mission even better."

St. Vincent Hospital and Health Care Center

The first Daughters of Charity in Indianapolis arrive in April of 1881. They soon established the first St. Vincent Infirmary with their own $34.77 and a gift of $50 from Bishop Silas Chatard, who had invited the Sisters to the city to minister to the sick and poor.

On April 26, 1881, four Daughters of Charity of St. Vincent de Paul arrived in Indianapolis, Indiana. They brought with them hope, faith, a willingness to help the poor, sick, and injured—and $34.77.

Their new home was less than modest, an empty seminary that became the St. Vincent Infirmary. Soon, there were fifty beds in full operation and the infirmary took a new name. St. Vincent Hospital became a reality.

During the first eight years of operation, St. Vincent Hospital treated 1,012 patients, one of whom stayed a full three years and whose total bill was $1,254.33. Total expenses for the hospital during that same period were $33,695.78.

A highlight of the early years was the admission, on September 23, 1902, of Theodore Roosevelt, then President of the United States. Mr. Roosevelt immediately recognized the men's unit supervisor, Sister Regina. She had served under him at Montauk Point, having cared for the fever-stricken men of Roosevelt's regiment of Rough Riders.

In 1918, a visitor of another sort came to St. Vincent, which had since moved to a new building on Fall Creek Parkway at Illinois Street. The "Spanish Flu" crowded the hospital with patients. During that fall, most of the Sisters were ill and thirty-six of the eighty medical students were down with "la grippe," which killed 445,000 people in the United States in four months.

Since that time, many changes have occurred in medicine and at St. Vincent. But throughout this century, St. Vincent's philosophy of service to the sick and poor has remained the same. Out of this philosophy, specialized programs continued to emerge to meet the intensifying needs of people in a society growing more complex. Today, St. Vincent Hospitals and Health Services encompasses:

St. Vincent Hospital and Health Care Center, a world-renowned 617-bed hospital, opened in 1974.

St. Vincent Family Life Center, where approximately 3,500 babies are born each year. It opened adjacent to St. Vincent Hospital in 1984.

St. Vincent Stress Center, since 1982 a unique specialty hospital offering programs in mental health, chemical dependency, and hospice. Other services include home health care, a learning support center for the learning disadvantaged, and employee assistance programs.

St. Vincent Carmel Hospital, a five-year-old, 100-bed hospital offering the Hamilton County area the services of a major medical facility with twenty-four-hour emergency services, all private rooms, a highly skilled medical staff, and a surgery department with state-of-the-art equipment.

St. Vincent New Hope, opened in 1978 to provide residential rehabilitation and habilitation services for 200 young adults with congenital or acquired disabilities. New Hope also operates group homes and the Neuro Rehab Center for people with brain injuries or other neurological disorders.

St. Vincent is a strong, viable, and successful presence in the health care community. However, a healthy financial picture is not the only goal. The first concerns must be that the ill and injured are cared for properly and that programs are underway to keep people well. This emphasis on care means focusing resources on education and research, services for the poor, and innovative programs, regardless of their short-term payback. St. Vincent remains committed to helping people achieve their highest potential through mental, physical, and spiritual health and development.

That is the cornerstone of the mission and ministry of healing of the Daughters of Charity.

This hospital on Fall Creek Parkway housed St. Vincent for 61 years, 1913-1974.

Union Federal Savings Bank

Union Federal Savings Bank was founded in 1887 as the Indianola Building and Loan Association, with its office at 1402 West Washington Street. In 1933, the office was moved to 148 East Market Street. The institution was converted to a Federal Savings and Loan Association in 1937 and moved to 137 East Market Street that same year. Rapid growth forced another move in 1941, this time to 160 East Market Street. In 1947, as growth continued, Union Federal asked permission to open a branch office. The following year, Union Federal opened the first savings and loan branch in the city at 7 East Maple Road.

Assets of the Association were increased by more than $11 million in 1959 when Union Federal merged with Colonial Savings and Loan Association. In 1962, Union Federal announced plans to construct a new building on the corner of Pennsylvania and Market Streets. By 1964, the new facility was completed. The building still houses much of Union Federal's management operations today, as well as its main branch.

Artist rendering of Union Federal Savings Bank, 1985

Union Federal Savings Bank, 45 N. Pennsylvania Street, 1964

In 1981, Union Federal opened its first Marsh Supermarket branch at Sixty-second and Allisonville Road, with the hope of offering customers one-stop banking and grocery shopping. Today, Union Federal has eleven Marsh Supermarket branches throughout the Indianapolis area.

In September of 1984, Union Federal was acquired by the principals of Waterfield Mortgage Co. With this acquisition came an expansive mortgage banking operation, leading Union Federal to become a leader in home financing.

The acquisition brought a rush of growth to Union Federal. The first evidence came in late 1985 when the downtown Union Federal building underwent extensive renovation, including a new reflective glass exterior, a remodeled lobby area, and new modular work stations.

In January of 1986, Union Federal Savings requested and was granted permission from the Federal Home Loan Bank Board to change its name to Union Federal Savings Bank. As a savings bank, Union Federal could offer its customers a full range of banking services.

Union Federal vastly expanded its operations in 1987 with the acquisition of Community Federal Savings and Loan Association of Ohio. With the addition of Community Federal's twelve branches, Union Federal became the largest federal savings bank in Indiana, with assets of approximately $1.2 billion and thirty-three branch offices in Indiana and Ohio.

Union Holding, parent of Union Federal Savings Bank, grew in 1988 with the acquisition of Arsenal Savings Association, F.A., Indianapolis, and Frankton Federal Savings and Loan Association. Arsenal, with eight branches, was renamed Union Federal Savings Bank of Indianapolis, while Frankton's single branch was renamed Union Federal Savings Bank of Frankton.

Union Federal is one of the largest federal savings banks in Indiana with assets of $1.3 billion as of December 31, 1989.

Walker Research, Inc.

Walker's corporate headquarters, located at 3939 Priority Way S. Dr., contains 90,000 square feet housing professionals dedicated to serving business information needs for clients throughout the world.

Walker Research began modestly in 1939, on the dining room table of the Walker family home in Indianapolis. Mrs. Dorothy "Tommie" Walker had heard about a part-time job that would be ideal for earning extra income for her family. The job was a telephone survey for a local bank. It paid fifty cents an hour.

It didn't take long for Tommie Walker's job to grow into a business. Although she had completed only four research studies that first year, she had launched a career in an industry she would often refer to as the oldest of arts and newest of sciences.

By 1949, the first away-from-home office was opened in a converted garage on East 62nd Street. Surveys conducted in those days reflect an earlier time, including research on consumer acceptance of home television sets and travel preferences between the early airlines and the railroads.

In 1957, a house was purchased on East 46th Street and converted into the first consumer test center operated by an independent marketing research company. The idea of bringing in groups of respondents to a center was so successful that

expansion to a second center soon became necessary.

By 1962, added capabilities enabled the firm to provide much more than interviewing. Walker employees could design the research study, write questionnaires, collect data from consumers, tabulate the results (by hand), and write, print, and deliver a final report.

The company was incorporated in 1964 and remains a privately-held company today. In 1965, the company moved to a building at 2809 East 56th Street which had been designed for its exclusive use.

During the late sixties, large shopping centers and enclosed malls began to dot the suburban landscape. Walker was eager to gather opinions in that new environment and started interviewing at Lafayette Square. Soon afterward, Walker first expanded outside the Indianapolis market and opened a branch office in a suburban St. Louis mall.

In the 1970s, as the use of survey research grew rapidly, some consumer resistance toward research was identified. Walker devised a "Your Opinion Counts" campaign to promote the benefits of research

and aid consumers' understanding of it. Walker offered the use of the slogan to the research industry, and it has become an industry logo.

During 1975, the corporate offices moved to 8000 Knue Road in the Castleton Office Park. As a result of growth, in late 1985 all Indianapolis-based staff relocated to a new four-story national headquarters building in the northside Precedent Office Park located near the intersection of I-465 and Highway 431. The 90,000-square-foot headquarters building was especially designed for Walker.

In 1986, an affiliated organization, Walker Clinical Evaluations, Inc., was founded. This company conducts clinical investigations and trials with human subjects related to products and devices which are controlled by the Food and Drug Administration. In 1987, Walker Research, Inc., initiated a defined division concept, which in 1990 resulted in the creation of three separate business units:

Walker: Research & Analysis, a full-service custom ad hoc research organization. Branch offices are located in the New York, Cincinnati, and San Francisco metropolitan areas.

Walker: Customer Satisfaction Measurements, a quality improvement consulting firm that relies heavily on research data. Branch functions are located in New York and Phoenix.

Walker: DataSource, a data collection and data processing organization which also offers a variety of database and computer services. In addition to several facilities in Indianapolis, the division operates offices in Tampa, Cincinnati, Ft. Wayne, and Phoenix.

Walker's businesses are "people" businesses. Today the combined family of businesses employ nearly 1,000 nationwide. These units have emerged as some of the nation's largest and fastest growing marketing research and information firms. Walker works for an impressive list of clients, for which it is thankful and proud.

The Indiana Historical Society (IHS), the oldest historical society west of the Allegheny Mountains, was founded on December 11, 1830 and chartered by the Indiana General Assembly the following month. Many of the most distinguished figures in Indiana's early history attended the organizational meeting and agreed that the objectives of the organization would be "the collection and preservation of all materials calculated to shed light on the natural, civil, and political history of Indiana; the publication and circulation of historical documents; the promotion of useful knowledge; and the friendly and profitable intercourse of such citizens of the state as are disposed to promote the aforesaid objectives." Adjusted to changing times and circumstances, these words continue to guide the destiny of IHS in the 1990s.

Between 1830 and 1886, officers convened IHS membership meetings in only twelve years. The Indiana General Assembly sporadically appropriated small sums, but, before the nineteenth century was out, the IHS officers all but gave up on this source of revenue. In 1886, however, IHS stabilized as a membership organization. Since then members have met at least annually and publications have appeared regularly.

When Delavan Smith (1861-1922) willed a collection of books and $150,000 to honor his father (William Henry Smith, founder of the Associated Press), IHS acquired the wherewithal to commence its library function. By 1933, the William Henry Smith Memorial Library opened its doors within the new State Library Historical Building and the library developed during ensuing decades.

So did the research and publications programs. IHS began publishing solid, readable books, including a Pulitzer Prize winner in 1950, *The Old Northwest: Pioneer Period, 1815-1840* by R. Carlyle Buley. A long shelf of books appeared during the 1950s, 60s, and 70s and established IHS as a publisher of useful monographs, regional documentary material, and studies of native Americans.

At this point IHS's principal benefactor and longtime member of the board of trustees, Eli Lilly (1885-1977), stepped forward. He provided capital funds to enable the Society in 1976 to move its collection and eleven-member staff into a new addition to the Indiana State Library and Historical Building that provided 17,000 square feet of space. In addition, Mr. Lilly willed a portion of his estate to IHS. The resulting endowment income made possible unprecedented institutional growth during the 1980s.

In the 1990s, the Indiana Historical Society operates under its original charter as a not-for-profit corporation. A board of eighteen trustees establishes policies for the central administration, three divisions (library, publications, and field services), satellite projects, a full-time staff of fifty, and an active membership of 8,000.

The William Henry Smith Memorial Library is a growing, research-oriented repository of more than 60,000 books and pamphlets; 3,500 manuscript and archive collections; 1,500,000 photographs and pictures; 1,000 maps; and significant ancillary material relating to the history of Indiana and the Old Northwest. In its formative years, the library confined its collecting to ante-bellum Indiana and the Old Northwest. An expanded collecting focus now includes both nineteenth and twentieth-century history with particular emphasis on agricultural, architectural, black, ethnic, medical, military, transportation, women's, and the social history of Indiana.

Publications remain a mainstay of the IHS dissemination program. New books are published annually. IHS also produces a newsletter and an illustrated quarterly, *Traces of Indiana and Midwestern History.* As annual benefits, members receive both periodicals, at least one book, plus the quarterly *Indiana Magazine of History* published at Indiana University. Members may also affiliate with any two IHS interest groups (Archaeology, Black History, Family History, and Medical History) and receive their publications as well. These are: *Prehistory Research Series, Black History News and Notes, The Hoosier Genealogist,* and *Snakeroot Extract.*

Through its Field Services Division IHS organizes three Indiana history conferences each year, conducts workshops and consultant programs for county and local historical societies, circulates traveling exhibitions, administers the Fort Knox II site in Vincennes, and co-sponsors a county historian program.

Other IHS activities include recording material for the print-handicapped with a volunteer force, microfilming Indiana newspapers, providing funds for the Indiana Junior Historical Society, producing exhibitions and radio programs, offering dissertation fellowships, extending grants, and funding projects.

Bibliography

The Indianapolis Chamber of Commerce has kept very good records during the hundred years of its history. The earliest materials (including the first decade, with some committee minutes that extend into the 1930s) are housed in the Indiana Historical Society Library. Their Library also has extensive collections of photographs illustrating the commercial history of Indianapolis, including photographs from the Chamber of Commerce and from the most important of the early commercial photographers, the Bass Company.

The Chamber has maintained a complete record of its official board minutes and annual reports. It also has a complete file of its two major magazines, *Activities* and *Indianapolis Magazine*. Additionally, many committee minutes, informational and promotional materials, and some internal records have survived.

Many of the Chamber's activities were reported over the years in the pages of Indianapolis newspapers, which sometimes contain livelier accounts than can be found in the official record. Complete microfilm collections of *The Indianapolis News* (a founding member of the Indianapolis Chamber) and of *The Indianapolis Star* can be found at both the Indianapolis- Marion County Public Library and the Indiana State Library.

The history of the city until 1910, including the early years of the Commercial Club, can be found well documented in Jacob Piatt Dunn's *Greater Indianapolis*. Much less has been written on Indianapolis in the remainder of the twentieth century, an omission that will soon be corrected by *Polis: An Encyclopedia of Indianapolis,* a forthcoming project sponsored by Indiana University-Purdue University at Indianapolis.

EDITOR'S NOTE: To preserve the historical accuracy and authenticity of this book, all quotes have been left intact as originally written or reported. No effort has been made to adapt them to fit the editorial style of the book.

Photo Credits

The ability to reproduce photographic and other illustrative material is gratefully acknowledged. The following four organizations were instrumental in providing appropriate art for this book, and because of the wealth of material used from their archives, will be abbreviated as follows:

IHS—Indiana Historical Society Library
BASS—Bass Photo Collection, Indiana
    Historical Society
ISL—Indiana State Library, Indiana Division
ICC—Indianapolis Chamber of Commerce
    Archives

Color Section
Page
2-3   Richard Listenberger
4-5   *Harper's Weekly,* August 11, 1888
6-7   Top left, right and inset: McGuire Studios, Inc.;
      Bottom: Michael Vaughn
  8   McGuire Studios, Inc.

Chapter One
Page
10   Top: IHS, Bass #31197; Bottom: Cecil Beeson
11   ISL, Newspaper Division
12   IHS, Bass #298536
13   Top: Eli Lilly and Company Archives; Middle: ICC;
      Bottom: ICC
14   Eli Lilly and Company Archives
15   Eli Lilly and Company Archives
16   Top: ICC; Bottom: Eli Lilly and Company Archives
17   Top: ISL; Bottom: Richard Listenberger
18   IHS, Bass #4398
19   ICC
20   IHS, Bass #16326
21   ICC
22   IHS, Bass #17805
23   Bottom: IHS, ICC Coll.
24   Oddessey Map Store
25   Top: Dan M. Mitchell; Bottom: IHS, ICC Coll.
26   IHS, Bass #91483
27   IHS, Bass #91483

Chapter Two
Page
28   IHS #6487
29   Bottom: ISL
30   Top left: IHS, Bass #69855; Top right: IHS, Bass
      #66449-F; Bottom: IHS, Bass #30145
31   Middle: IHS, ICC Coll.; Bottom: IHS, Bass
      #87718-F
32   Top: IHS, Medical History Museum; Bottom: ISL,
      American Lung Association of Central Indiana
33   Top: IHS, Medical History Museum; Middle: ISL,
      American Lung Association of Central Indiana;
      Bottom: IHS, ICC Coll.
34   IHS, Bass #287788
35   Top: ISL; Bottom: ISL, ICC Coll.
36   ISL
37   Middle: ISL; Bottom: ICC
38   IHS, Madame C.J. Walker Coll.
39   Middle: IHS, ICC Coll.; Bottom: ISL, ICC Coll.
40   IHS, Bass #24898
41   Bottom: IHS, ICC Coll.
42   ISL
44   Top: IHS, Bass #24464; Bottom: IHS, Bass
      #27393
45   Top: ISL, ICC Coll.; Bottom: Richard Listenberger
46   Top: United Way of Central Indiana; Bottom: IHS,
      Bass #60776-F
47   Top: ICC Coll.; Bottom: 500 Festival Associates
48   IHS, Bass #66384
49   IHS, Bass #66384
50   ICC
51   ICC

Chapter Three
Page
52   IHS, Bass #97886
53   Top: Indianapolis Newspapers, Inc.; Bottom: IHS
      #C4303
54   IHS, Bass #71783
55   ISL, ICC Coll.
56   ISL, ICC Coll.
57   Middle: ICC; Bottom: ISL, ICC Coll.
58   Top: IHS, Bass; Bottom: IHS, Bass #C516
59   Top: ICC; Bottom: IHS, Bass #70645
60   IHS, Bass #74097
61   ICC
62   IHS, Bass #75587
63   Top: IHS, Bass #99642; Bottom: ISL

Photos in the Partners in Progress Section provided by the individual businesses.

Acknowledgments

The Indianapolis Chamber of Commerce is deeply indebted to many individuals in the compilation of its history and the creation of this book, particularly George and Miriam Geib for capturing the spirit of the Chamber and its role in the development of Indianapolis, Carl Dortch and committee for their advisement, Melba Hopper for laboring long hours in researching and compiling visuals, and Richard Listenberger for his work in bringing it all together.

Without assistance from the Indiana Historical Society, the publication of *Indianapolis First* would not have been possible. Special thanks are in order to Susan Sutton, the Society's coordinator of visual services, and Marybelle Burch Teloso, formerly of the Indiana State Library, for their assistance in compiling historical photographs and their dedication of numerous hours to the project.

The Indianapolis Chamber is also sincerely indebted to twenty-three member companies for the financial resources necessary to bring this history from manuscript to publication. They include: The Associated Group; Baker & Daniels; BANK ONE, INDIANAPOLIS, NA; Barnes & Thornburg; Business Furniture Corporation; Citizens Gas & Coke Utility; Community Hospitals Indianapolis; Ice Miller Donadio and Ryan; INB National Bank; The Indianapolis News; Indianapolis Power and Light Company; Jenn-Air Company; Lacy Diversified Industries, Ltd.; Eli Lilly and Company; Marsh Supermarkets; Merchants National Bank and Trust Company; Park Fletcher, Inc.; Railroadmen's Federal Savings and Loan Association; Ransburg Corporation; St. Francis Hospital Center; St. Vincent Hospital and Health Care Center; Union Federal Savings Bank; and Walker Research, Inc.

Also, the Chamber is grateful to Thomas Rumer, a local freelance writer who provided a wealth of knowledge about early photos; Jack Evans, historian for Allison Transmission Divison of General Motors Corporation; Robert L. Eakins, United Way of Central Indiana; Edward J. Zebrowski, Sr.; William L. Selms, historian for Indianapolis Historic Preservation Commission; the library staff of Indianapolis Newspapers, Inc., particularly Beatrice G. Shepard; Donald Merchant, an aviation history expert; Cal Burleson of the Indianapolis Indians; and Herbert O. Fisher, a past staff member of the Chamber and a leader in aviation technology.

The Chamber also extends its appreciation to Fort Benjamin Harrison, particularly to Marilyn Kindard, historian, and John Kandt, public affairs director; the Madame Walker Urban Life Center, particularly Kathy Hazelwood; Kathleen McDonnel of the Medical History Library; Ron McQueeney, photo director of the Indianapolis Motor Speedway Museum; and Anita Martin, historian for Eli Lilly and Company.

Also due appreciation for their efforts in the compilation of this history are Mary Burchard of 500 Festival Associates; William Campbell of Allison Gas and Turbine Division; McCord Purdy, an early automobile "buff," for the inclusion of several pieces from his collection; IUPUI Archives, particularly Eric Pomroy, head of special collections and archives; and the Benjamin Harrison Memorial Home.

The Indianapolis Chamber of Commerce particularly acknowledges those individuals that served on volunteer committees and contributed tremendously to the planning and execution of its 100th anniversary celebration.

100th Anniversary Commission: John Burkhart (Chairman), Thomas W. Binford, Alexander S. Carroll, Richard B. DeMars, Carl R. Dortch, Eugene B. Hibbs, Boris E. Meditch, Andrew J. Paine, Jr., James W. Parks, Fred C. Tucker, Jr., and Frank D. Walker.

Commemorative Book Committee: Carl R. Dortch (Chairman), James E. Farmer, George Geib, Miriam Geib, Carl Henn, the late Frank Hoke, and Anita Martin.

Steering Committee: Robert Gildea, Sid Weedman (Co-Chairmen), Hugh J. Baker III, Bob Clark, Ron Carrell, Tom Dingledy, Dave Goodrich, Tom Hirschauer, Mary Huggard, Karl Kalp, Virginia Merkel, David Shank, Betsy Spalding, and Judy Waugh.

Most importantly, due special recognition is the extremely professional and dedicated staff serving the Chamber at the time of its 100th anniversary. Their hard work and enthusiasm are hereby acknowledged.

Executive: Thomas A. King, president; John S. Myrland, executive vice president; Santina C. Sullivan, vice president; Karen D. Wright, executive assistant, and Kelli L. Riley, executive assistant.

Government Affairs: Rebecca L. Hopewell, government affairs director; Martin S. Dezelan, government affairs manager, and Suzy B. Faulkner, administrative assistant.

Community Affairs: Kerri E. Randel, manager, community affairs; Andrea L. Marshall, community affairs specialist; Linda D. Paul, community affairs specialist; Cynthia R. Stout, P.I.E. project manager; Anne L. Rogers, P.I.E. partnership coordinator; Suzette M. Brown, SKL alumni coordinator; Judy Zimmerman, administrative assistant; L. Kathleen Brown, P.I.E. administrative assistant, and Christina L. Fulk, administrative assistant.

Special Services: Robert H. Stone, special services director.

Administration: Karen T. Poulsen, director of financial services; Cheryl J. Wright, manager, adminstrative services, and Jennifer M. Jones, accounting assistant.

Member Services: Lee Lewellen, director, business research; Jeffery L. Barnett, manager, business information and small business; Steven L. Campbell, manager, business research; Susan J. Lloyd, administrative assistant; Beth A. Willever, administrative assistant, and Carrie J. Harney, community information/receptionist.

Membership and Marketing: Beverly M. Farra, director, membership and marketing; Tamara S. Palmer, manager, membership development; Jeanette B. Claffey, manager, membership relations, and Linda S. McKinley, administrative assistant.

Communications: Daniel J. Fenton, communications director; Lauri J. Hogan, communications manager, and Margery A. Martin, administrative assistant.

166

Index

**INDIANAPOLIS
CHAMBER
OF COMMERCE**

INDIANAPOLIS
CHAMBER
OF COMMERCE